The Complete POODLE CLIPPING and GROOMING BOOK

by SHIRLEE KALSTONE

Illustrations by MARTY WOLFSON
Photographs by LARRY KALSTONE

SECOND EDITION
Second Printing—1982

HOWELL BOOK HOUSE Inc.
230 Park Avenue, New York, N.Y. 10169

Acknowledgments

I WISH TO EXPRESS MY GRATITUDE to the following people and (in many instances) their dogs: Mrs. Russell Coneby and Apricot Brandy of Lougean; Evelyn Yalch and Yalcher's Flame 'N Candle, Yalcher's Tangerine D'Roux and Merrymorn Lorelei; Janet Dancy and Edris Scene Stealer and Jaycee Sunny New Dawn; Racille Karelitz and Racille's Jamie of Stoneleigh and La Plush Petite; John Nash of The Nash Academy of Animal Arts; Loretta Vogt; Paule Vuye of Brussels, Belgium; Kathe Winther of Copenhagen, Denmark, and to my own Poodles: Edris Quick Deal, Stoneleigh Dealer's Choice, Stoneleigh Serendipity and Stoneleigh Sparkle Farkle. I want to especially thank the exhibitors and their dogs who were photographed from ringside in this country and abroad, and also the people who were kind enough to allow us to photograph their Poodles' faults.

—S.K.

Library of Congress Cataloging in Publication Data

Kalstone, Shirlee.
   The complete poodle clipping and grooming book.

   1. Poodles. 2. Dogs—Grooming. I. Wolfson, Marty.
II. Kalstone, Larry. III. Title.
SF429.P85K3 1981   636.7'2   81-6905
ISBN 0-87605-267-7   ACCR2

Contents

THE SHOW CLIPS

THE PET CLIPS

A Standard Poodle in Continental Clip being examined by a judge in the show ring.

Introduction

THE COMPLETE POODLE CLIPPING AND GROOMING BOOK is written for Poodle owners who would like to clip and care for their own dogs, as well as for professionals. Anyone who owns a Poodle and is genuinely interested in learning how to clip can set patterns and learn how to scissor by careful study of the instructions on the following pages.

Whatever variety you own, Poodles require much more attention than most other breeds. They must be brushed, bathed and clipped regularly, for if they are not cared for, they become shaggy. Regular grooming is important not only to make a Poodle look better, but also for its good health and mental fitness. Most professionals will agree that when a dog is groomed regularly, it is less likely to suffer from mats and tangles, skin problems, ear infections, overgrown toenails, or infestation by external parasites. In addition, Poodles are proud animals. They know when they look their best and really enjoy the praise people give them when they appear perfectly groomed. Poodle personalities hide under a shaggy coat!

This book concentrates on the art of clipping and setting patterns. There are instructions for the show clips recognized by The American Kennel Club and for numerous popular pet clips. Pet Poodles can be trimmed into hundreds of different styles or variations. Some of them are grotesque, attempting to make the elegant Poodle look like a monkey or other farcical object. *Such clips are not included in this book!* Throughout the book, you will notice that the accent is placed on giving a professional finish to all clips. This is done by good scissoring, a task that requires a great deal of practice, and when perfected makes the difference between a mediocre job and a really artistic clip. If you can scissor well and are familiar with the Poodle Standard, you can make a structurally sound Poodle look like perfection and minimize glaring faults on a Poodle that is not so sound.

To be a good groomer, you must first know what a good Poodle looks like. Before you trim a Poodle, always examine it. If the dog is near-perfect, wonderful! Your job is to trim the dog attractively. A structurally sound Poodle looks well in any style clip, if it is done correctly. But can you tell if your Poodle is sound? Can you determine if your dog has a fault? If he does, there are ways to camouflage many imperfections. An excellent groomer can make an average Poodle look much finer than a perfect Poodle clipped by a mediocre groomer.

Whether you use this book to learn to clip your own dog or to eventually become a professional, first familiarize yourself with the description of the ideal of the breed. This book contains simplified explanations of the Poodle Standard, photographs showing rights and wrongs, and some grooming tips to disguise glaring faults. If you study them well, you should eventually be able to determine what must be done to make each dog look good.

Remember, nothing will help you to become an expert groomer more than practice. If you are a beginner, spend at least a few minutes each day working on your dog, even if it means only brushing and combing. Dogs can sense inexperience by the way they are handled, and your dog may try every trick to discourage you when you first begin clipping. Be firm and in control, but at the same time, treat your Poodle with kindness. It is never necessary to slap or otherwise mistreat your dog to force him to behave while he is on the grooming table. If you are mean to the dog, he will immediately resent you and will never cooperate because he will associate grooming with an unpleasant experience.

By working on your dog a few minutes each day, you will pick up speed in your scissoring and find that you are beginning to handle your clipper like a professional. Suddenly, you find your Poodle has confidence in you and stops fussing. He realizes the more he cooperates with you, the faster the clipping goes.

Good luck to all prospective groomers. When your Poodle walks beside you, impeccably groomed, and someone asks who clipped him, what more satisfying answer can you give than *"I did it myself!"*

The Development of Poodle Trimming

THE POODLE is a very ancient breed. There is some controversy over its origins, although most cynologists believe that it originated in Eastern Germany or Russia. Whatever its native land, the Poodle was known in many European countries, and as far back as the breed can be traced, trimming has been a continued practice. Poodles in lion trims appear on ancient Greek and Roman coins, and in the time of Emperor Augustus, around 30 A.D., they were carved on monuments and tombs, resembling, in a primitive way, their modern day counterparts.

Clipped Poodles are conspicuous in Medieval illuminated manuscripts; 15th century engravings by Albrecht Durer; and paintings from the 15th, 16th, and 17th centuries, most notably, two scenes of *The Story of Patient Grisdelda* by Pintoricchio (1454-1513); *Tobit and His Dog* by Martin de Vos (1531-1603), and *The Dancing Dog* by Jan Steen (1626-79). Steen, who delighted in painted animated scenes of merrymaking, has given us one of the most charming representations of a Miniature Poodle. As a young boy plays a flute, the Poodle dances on his hind legs in a tavern courtyard, while smiling guests and servants enjoy the scene. The dog's hindquarters are clipped and he sports a ring of hair and a pompon on his tail.

Numerous authorities believe that the Poodle is closely related to or was the old Water Dog or *Canis familiaris aquaticus.* Early canine historians such as Dr. Caius (1570), Conrad Gessner (1553), Edward Topsell (1607), Gervaise Markham (1621), Aldrovandus (published posthumously in 1637), and Cirino (1653), write about and show crude wood-cuts of a water dog with clipped hindquarters and a tuft of hair at the end of the tail. The Standard is the oldest of the three varieties and authorities agree that the Poodle was used in Europe for centuries to retrieve game from water. Stonehenge, the great 19th century British cynologist, describes the Poodle as the favorite water dog of continental fowlers in France, Belgium, Holland, Denmark, Germany and Russia. There can be no doubt that the Poodle's name in different languages suggests a water dog: *Pudel* (his German name) comes from the verb *Pudelin,* meaning to splash in water, and *Caniche* (his French name) is a derivation of *Canard Chien,* or duck dog.

The long-practice custom of shaving the hindquarters undoubtedly evolved because the Poodle's coat was somewhat of a hindrance in the water. The area behind the ribs was trimmed smooth to facilitate efficient swimming. On the shaved hindquarters, small tufts of hair were left to cover the joints and keep them warm. The long hair over the neck, shoulders, ribs, and chest protected the heart and added a buoyancy while swimming. When the dog emerged from the water with his quarry, the thick woolly mane coat provided warmth. The later fashion of tying up the topknot was also related to the Poodle's retrieving work. The dog could see his quarry better when his forelocks were fastened above the head, instead of falling into his eyes, so owners began to use pieces of brightly colored ribbon to tie back the long hair. This custom also permitted an owner to locate or follow a particular dog as it worked in the water.

"The perfect Water Dogge,'' woodcut engraving from Gervaise Markham's book *Hungers Prevention*, London 1621. Note bird in the dog's mouth.

The first printed reference to trimming was in 1621, in *Hunger's Prevention or The Arte of Fowling by Water and Lande* by Gervaise Markham, a book describing the use and training of Water Dogges. Markham tells us:

> "Now for the cutting and shaving him from the Navill downward, or backward, it is two wayes well to be allowed of, that is, for Sommer hunting or for the water; because these Water Dogges naturally are ever most laden with haires on the hinder parts, nature as it were labouring to defend that part most....and because the hinder parts are ever deeper in the water than the fore parts, therefore nature hath given them the greatest armour of haire to defend the wette and coldness; yet this defence in Sommer time by the violence of the heate of the Sunne, and the greatnesse of the Dogges labor is very noysome and troublesome...."

"And so likewise in the matter of water, it is a very heavy burthen to the Dogge and makes him to swimme lesse nimbly and slower....But for the cutting or shaving of a Dogge all quite over from the Foote to the Nostrill, that I utterly dislike, for it not only takes from the generall benefits which Nature hath lent him, but also brings such a tendernesse and chilnesse all over his body, that the water in the end will grow Yrksome unto him...."

Markham includes a woodcut of such a trimmed dog (see illustration) with bird in mouth, and describes it as "the perfect Water Dogge."

Although Poodles originally were trimmed for occupational and hygienic reasons, when it became the custom to trim them into more outlandish styles, the flair of the French emerged. During the reign of Louis XVI (1774-92), the art of Poodle trimming became extremely decorative. Dog barbers worked along the banks of the Seine and in the streets of Paris, and no clip was too outrageous or difficult for them to perfect. The barbers cut out coats of arms, lovers' knots, monograms, and fleurs-de-lis in the Poodles' hair and ornamented them (see illustration) with moustaches and imperiales (small pointed beards on the underjaw), or high pompadours similar to those worn by ladies of the royal court.

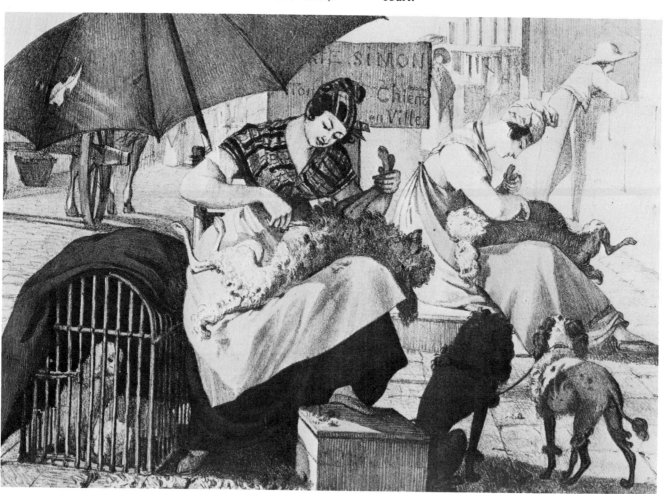

Clipped Poodles appear in 18th century English engravings and paintings resembling their French cousins. Poodle trimming became more popular in England as the years passed and, by Victorian times, it was a full-time occupation for some.

In the past, the Poodle was divided into two varieties—corded and curly—the difference being one of coat type. The corded Poodle's coat hung in long, coarse ringlets from the body, ears and tail. The cords, often more than 18 inches long, covered the front legs like a skirt when they hung naturally to the ground. To keep them from dragging along and attracting dirt, the cords were often tied up in bundles with leather straps or ribbons over the dog's back. A great deal of time was devoted to maintaining the cords. They were seldom bathed, but had to be oiled frequently to keep the long ends from becoming brittle and snapping off. Writers of the times sometimes described corded Poodles as "offending the nostrils."

In 1891, *The American Book of the Dog* by G. O. Shields included one of the first diagrams for clipping the Poodle "in the style generally adopted in England and which is best adapted to showing off the dog to the greatest advantage." Shields describes the Poodle's cords as being "about the thickness of a crow quill" and adds that "the entire coat, from the base of the skull to the root of the tail, should divide evenly down the back, showing a clearly defined parting, and should touch the ground completely, hiding the forelegs and feet, and thus, combining with the cords from the throat and chest, give the dog the appearance of being in petticoats. The coat should cord all over the body, except in the eyebrows, moustache and imperiale, which should be straight, even without wave, and of a

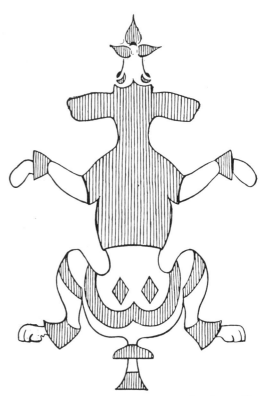

Early diagram for clipping the Poodle, from *The American Book of the Dog* by G. O. Shields, 1891.

glossier texture than the rest of the coat. The cords on the ears should reach far down on the shoulders, and so mingle with those of the neck as to render the ears nearly undistinguishable. On the head, the cords should fall away from the center, leaving a well-defined crown, and should have no tendency to stand erect, like those of a Water Spaniel."

Corded Poodles made their debut in the British show ring in 1876 and occupied a commanding position at dog shows in England and on the continent for years. They must have been the "darlings" of newsmen of the day as they are described and portrayed frequently in popular magazines and newspapers. Rawdon Lee describes a Poodle in 1899, named Fairy Queen, shown by an Englishwoman from Leeds: "This was a white dog and its cords were of such length that they were many inches longer than the height of the animal. When lying at rest, a close examination had to be made to discern which was the head and which the stern of this curious creature." Lee mentions another large Poodle of the day, named Lyris, 21½ inches high at the shoulders, whose cords measured 37 inches from tip to tip, as well as his son, Achilles, standing 23 inches high at the shoulders with cords 30 inches long, falling 6 inches below his feet.

The corded Poodle has all but disappeared, but once in a while, one will appear in a show ring some-

A typical corded coat Poodle, reproduced from *The English Stockkeeper.* Corded Poodles occupied a commanding position at the dog shows in England and on the continent in the late 1800s.

"Nero," a famous German Poodle, as he appeared at the Berlin International Dog Show in 1880.

where in the world. The corded variety will long be remembered and has given us a precious legacy. Some of today's finest Poodles descend from the distinguished British corded bloodlines, from whom they undoubtedly inherit their lush coat textures.

Nineteenth century books offer some remarkable grooming advice. In *House Dogs and Sporting Dogs* (1861), John Meyrick advises that "a dog who is well brushed regularly seldom requires washing, and is never infested with vermin but if the dog is to be washed, let it be done with the yolks of eggs, and not with soap, which irritates the skin, inflames the eyes, and by temporarily depriving the skin of its natural oily secretion, makes the dog extremely liable to become chilled afterwards. The washing with the yolks of eggs may be managed as follows: let the dog stand in an empty tub, rub the yolks of two, four or more eggs by degrees into his coat, adding lukewarm water, a little at a time, until the dog is covered with a thick lather. When it is well rubbed in over the whole coat, pour clean warm water over the dog till the egg is entirely washed out."

Rawdon Lee advises in *Modern Dogs: Non-Sporting Division* (1899) that "the coat of a black Poodle has to be dressed with some emollient, and nothing is better for this purpose than a mixture composed of a quarter pound of Vaseline to a half-pint of paraffin. This should be put into a suitable receptacle, which is to be placed in a heated oven and kept there until the concoction is thoroughly blended. It may be scented with any perfume fancy suggests and must then be placed in a jar, kept covered, and applied when cold." And heaven help the 19th century dog with mange! One common remedy (included in *Dogs: Their Origin and Varieties* by H. D. Richardson, 1860) was a mixture of one pint of train oil, one ounce of Turpentine, one ounce of naphtha, one ounce Oil of Tar, one ounce of soot, plus enough powdered sulphur to add consistency. This concoction was rubbed into the hair and had to remain there for three days!

TODAY, although most Poodles no longer retrieve for a living, two variations of the old Lion trim, the English Saddle and the Continental, with long mane coats over the shoulders, ribs and chest and shorter, scissored hindquarters, still remain the only acceptable adult trims for the show ring. A young Poodle may be shown in Puppy trim until 12 months of age, but then must be trimmed into either of the two other recognized styles.

The art of Poodle trimming has blossomed into a sophisticated profession throughout the world, especially in the United States. In addition to the traditional clips, there are hundreds of pet trims in which the Poodle's coat is clipped and scissored into various body patterns and leg styles. These are called "pet" trims because they are unacceptable in the conformation show ring.

Along with the many different clip styles, great advances in equipment and products have been made in the last few decades. The introduction of electric clippers for small animals, especially those with a variety of detachable blades which cut a Poodle's hair to various lengths have greatly simplified trimming for the breeder, exhibitor and groomer. Before that, groomers had to struggle with scissors and later, hand clippers which were time-consuming to use and often difficult to handle. The cutting action of the non-electric clippers worked on the same principle as a hedge-clipper, in which the opening and closing of the operator's hand controlled a small blade which cut the hair.

In addition to electric clippers and different blades to speed up the clipping process, a Poodle groomer can choose from different types of brushes and combs, making it possible to match grooming tools to each dog's coat type for more efficient grooming. The last 15 years has seen the introduction of fine shampoos, coat conditioners, tangle removers, rinses, grooming powders and insecticidal products—all formulated for more efficient and comfortable grooming for the groomer, but more importantly, for the dog.

10

How to Use
The Complete Poodle
Clipping and Grooming Book

IF YOU ARE A BEGINNER, plan to progress a little at a time. Before you attempt to do any clipping or scissoring, study the following suggestions:

1. Read and re-read the chapter on *Things to Remember*. This section sets the foundation to begin clipping and gives general information to help you understand and control your dog. Clipping can be easy and pleasant when you understand and observe a few simple rules.

2. Study the chapter *Suggestions About Equipment* carefully. To groom a Poodle, you need a clipper, a few extra blades which clip the hair to various lengths, a brush and comb, and a pair or two of fine quality barber scissors. Decide on the goal you want to reach. Do you eventually want to become a professional groomer? Then choose a clipper designed for professional work. Do you only want to clip your pet Poodle at home? In this case, select an inexpensive clipper—one not designed for heavy-duty professional use. Most beginners tend to overbuy equipment and before you purchase haphazardly, select the proper tools for the kind of work you plan to do.

3. Read the pages presenting the *Poodle Standard*. A breed Standard describes the ideal specimen, point by point, and is composed of sections defining General Appearance; head; neck; shoulder placement; body; hindquarters; legs and feet; tail; coat color and texture; size, and how the dog should gait. Put the sections together and you have a verbal image of the breed. Study the description of the ideal Poodle. Then examine the photographs and learn Poodle rights and wrongs. Study the accompanying Anatomy Chart. Poodle patterns are set by the bone structure of each dog. For this reason, not all Poodles are clipped in the same manner. To be a good groomer, first decide what a dog's faults are and what must be done to minimize these imperfections and make him look his best. Some clips are more flattering than others for dogs with major faults, while structurally sound dogs can be trimmed into any pattern.

4. Study the chapter on *Coat Care*. Brushing and combing should be the first actions you attempt. Before bathing, clipping and scissoring, your Poodle must be thoroughly brushed and combed out.

5. Examine the chapter on *Bathing and Maintenance*. Along with thorough brushing and combing, a correct shampoo, rinse, and fluff dry set the stage for the final clipping and scissoring.

6. Begin clipping the feet first since this will be the most troublesome area. Before you begin, study the correct way to clip the feet. Look at the photographs and illustrations in the clipping sections. To get the "feel" of your clipper, practice going over the feet once or twice without turning the motor on. Then, with your Poodle in the proper position on a sturdy table, with good light, begin slowly. If you are using clippers for the first time, remember to

hold the blade flat against the area you are clipping. Never point the blade into the skin. Don't be too concerned with getting a perfect job the first few times. Practice several minutes a day on the feet and your work will gradually improve as you go along. Feet are difficult at first because the dog senses your inexperience in handling this ticklish part of the body.

7. Trim the tail next. If you read the instructions carefully, clipping the tail should be no problem. Remember that the underside of the tail is a sensitive spot and subject to clipper burn. Don't use a fine blade on this area. When scissoring the pompon at the end of the tail, think of circles and balls, and try to trim a "round" rather than a "pine-tree" shape.

8. Clip the Poodle's face next. Study the instructions and photographs carefully. Then with your Poodle in position on the grooming table, begin clipping. Don't be concerned with getting an artistic finish the first few times you clip the face. This can be a very sensitive area and, if you are a beginner, don't try to progress too rapidly. Take your time. Try to gain the dog's confidence by being firm, *but never cross,* and practice the control tips when the dog begins to fuss.

9. Clip the neck according to directions. The underside of the neck and throat also are tender spots, subject to clipper burn. Never use a very fine blade on these areas.

10. Clip the stomach according to instructions.

11. The next stop is learning to scissor. If you are scissoring a Poodle for the first time, choose a simple clip like the Puppy, Kennel, Lamb, or Sporting to begin with. Follow instructions for the clip you select, and always work with the finest quality scissors you can afford. The real difference between amateur and professional trimming is in the scissoring. Don't try to set difficult patterns until you know how to scissor correctly.

12. Now you're ready to try pattern setting. Begin with one of the easy patterns, such as the Miami or New Yorker. Take your time! When you have gained confidence in your clipping ability and have mastered the easy patterns, try some difficult ones. Before selecting a pattern for your Poodle, remember to consider his size, conformation and coat texture. Poodles with good coat texture and no glaring structural faults look good in any clip, but fancy patterns are not for puppies or adult Poodles with soft coats, or major faults.

13. Each time you groom your Poodle, follow this clipping sequence:
    (a) Thoroughly brush and comb the dog to remove tangles.
    (b) Check the skin thoroughly for traces of external parasites or other problems.
    (c) Trim the tails.
    (d) Clean the ears.
    (e) Check the anal glands.
    (f) Shampoo the Poodle. If necessary, apply coat conditioner or insecticidal product.
    (g) Fluff dry the dog.
    (h) When the Poodle is dry, comb once again to fluff out the coat.
    (i) Clip feet, face and tail.
    (j) Do all body clipping (neck, stomach, and pattern).
    (k) Do body scissoring work. Scissor the back legs first, then work forward, trimming the hindquarters, back, ribs, shoulders, chest, and front legs.
    (l) Scissor the topknot. Do the ears and moustache (if applicable) last.

While professional groomers generally follow this step-by-step routine, most prefer to clip the feet, face, tail, and sometimes the body pattern in the "rough" before brushing and shampooing the dog. Clipping these areas beforehand does save time and help the Poodle to dry faster, but they must be reclipped after the dog is dry. If your Poodle has sensitive skin, you could cause clipper burn by clipping before the shampoo. The grooming method you select is a matter of personal preference. Remember that you must never do any major pattern clipping or scissoring on a dirty Poodle. Professionals achieve those velvety-looking results by working on clean hair.

14. Study the photographs and scissoring instructions on the Topknot Section before you scissor your Poodle's head. There are two basic topknot shapes. Whichever you select, the front of the topknot should be even with the eye. The mistake most beginners make is cutting off the hair in back of the eyes to keep it from falling forward.

ANATOMY OF THE POODLE

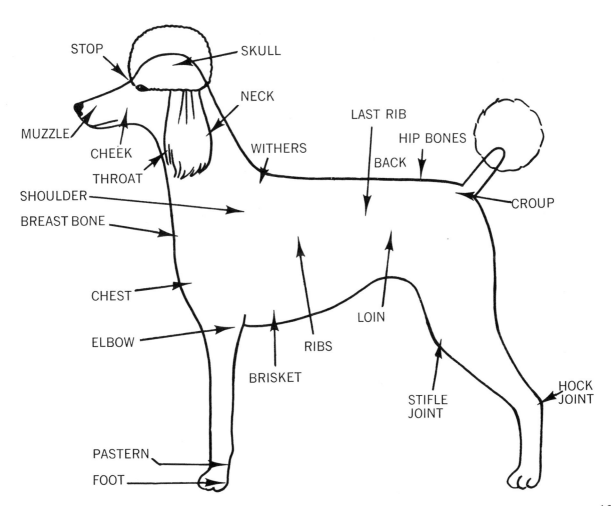

THINGS TO REMEMBER

1. Use the proper equipment. Read the *Suggestions about Equipment* chapter to become familiar with Poodle grooming tools, what each will do and how to use it correctly.

2. Good grooming behavior should be taught at an early age—and can be—if you remember two basic rules:
   (a) *Dogs learn by repetition, correction and praise.*
   (b) *Dogs should associate grooming with a pleasant experience.*
   This is a fine time to read obedience training books and learn the differences between positive and negative reinforcement.

3. Use a firm table for grooming. Because dogs learn by repetition, each time you brush or groom your Poodle, put him on the grooming table. Eventually, he will learn that he has to behave when he is being groomed. Never use an unsteady table—your dog will be frightened and try to jump off. Make sure your grooming table has a non-slip rubber top. If you own a Toy or Standard Poodle, for your own comfort, so that you won't have to bend over or stand on tip-toe, invest in an adjustable grooming table.

4. Groom in a room with adequate lighting. Have light coming from above and behind you. This is especially important when clipping dark-colored Poodles.

5. The grooming area should be quiet. Don't allow your Poodle to be distracted by other pets, children, or loud noises.

6. Begin grooming your Poodle while he is a puppy, if possible, and groom as often as possible.

7. Teach your Poodle to lie on his side while he is being brushed. This is important if the dog will be shown in the breed ring.

8. Don't expect your Poodle to stand perfectly still for hours on the grooming table when you first begin clipping. Young puppies have short periods of concentration and will not stand still very long. If your Poodle is young, plan no more than fifteen to twenty minutes of grooming at one time. A good way to begin table training is to stand the puppy on the table for brushing. Place your free hand under the stomach for support (and to give the dog confidence), then quickly run a brush through the coat. Speak quietly and reassuringly to the dog. At first, he may squirm about, but if you repeat this procedure every day for several weeks, he will learn to stand quietly and behave.

9. Learn to be firm during the grooming session, but not mean. Never slap or inhumanely treat your Poodle to make him behave on the grooming table. If he disobeys, correct him, and as soon as he does what you want, *praise him lavishly!* Use a firm tone of voice when making corrections, using a word such as "No" or "Stop," but always the same word so that your dog understands what you want him to do. Be consistent. Don't let your dog get away with something one day, then reprimand him for doing the same thing the next day.

10. Poodles are sensitive to voice inflections. If you lose patience, immediately stop what you are doing and let the dog off the table. Never let the dog associate grooming with an unpleasant experience. Postpone the session until another time if you think you're losing control.

11. Don't talk "baby talk" or play with your Poodle while he is on the grooming table. He's there to be groomed, not to play games. Reward him with lavish praise or a favorite treat after the grooming session.

12. If your Poodle is frightened by the sound of the clippers at first, hold him in your lap, rest the clippers near his back (with the motor running), speak quietly and reassuringly, and he will become accustomed to the noise.

13. Never bathe a matted Poodle. Always brush and comb the dog before shampooing. Don't neglect the hard-to-get areas under the front and back legs.

14. Don't clip or scissor a dirty Poodle. Working on dirty dogs dulls equipment quickly.

15. Never cut out mats from the Poodle's coat. If your dog is badly matted, follow suggestions found in the *Coat Care* chapter.

16. Learn to recognize clipper burn and how to treat it. Follow suggestions found in the special section on Clipper Burn.

17. Check for external parasites (fleas, ticks, etc.) before bathing. Instructions for ridding the dog of fleas and ticks are in the chapter on parasites in this book.

18. Never clip against the hair on the penis.

19. There are only two places where the skin must be stretched while clipping:
    (a) *The eyes*—To avoid cutting the open eye, use your thumb to stretch the corner of each eye upward and backward to close it completely.
    (b) *The muzzle*—To avoid cutting the fold of skin on each side of the mouth, use your thumb to stretch the corners of the lips back.

20. Use the edge of the clipper blade to clip along the lips.

21. When scissoring near the vulva or testicles, place your free hand over them for protection. There is no excuse for nicking a dog's genitals. The animal will never forget it and will not cooperate the next time he's groomed.

22. If your Poodle fusses and tries to raise the leg on which you are scissoring, lift the opposite leg with your free hand.

A handler scissors the pack and bracelets of a Miniature Poodle in English Saddle clip. Instructions for this trim begin on Page 81.

SUGGESTIONS ABOUT EQUIPMENT

NOW THAT YOU HAVE DECIDED to learn how to groom your Poodle, the next consideration is the selection of the necessary grooming equipment to do a thorough job. More importantly, while it is necessary to select the right grooming tools, you must know how to use them properly. Even the most basic tools, incorrectly used, can damage a dog's skin and hair. When correctly used, however, they can contribute significantly to the health of the skin and hair as well as to enhance the dog's general appearance. Listed below and clearly defined for easy selection are the various Poodle grooming tools. Study the various grooming instructions to determine *exactly* what you will need. Most beginners tend to overbuy equipment and without guidance, often select the wrong tools. One word of advice: whether you are interested in pet, show or professional grooming, *buy the best equipment you can afford.* Don't compromise on quality. The finest quality equipment lasts longer, saves time and, in the hands of someone knowledgeable, produces expert results.

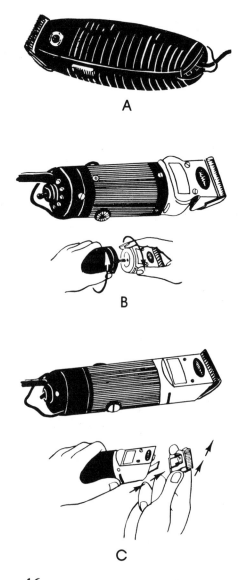

A

B

C

CLIPPERS

An electric clipper is necessary to clip the Poodle's hair. There are a number of excellent models to choose from and, usually, most are under a one year guarantee. Many models meet OSHA specifications (as set forth in the Occupational Safety and Health Act). Some clippers are designed for home grooming while others are constructed for heavy-duty professional use. When a clipper is to be used in a kennel or grooming salon, it is important that it be durable and well-balanced and that a number of blades be available that can be changed quickly.

While there are a number of electric clippers manufactured by various companies, Oster clippers seem to be the most popular and widely used for dog trimmng. The prospective groomer can choose from three basic models: the 113, also called the Lucky Dog Clipper (**A**) with detachable blades; the Model A-2, with detachable heads that click on and off by a simple twisting motion (**B**), and the Model A-5, with detachable blades that are easily snapped on or off by pressing a button at the base of the clipper (**C**). Although the A-2 has detachable cutter heads, the blades on these heads must be changed by using a screw driver. Because of the ease in changing blades on the A-5 clipper, it is the best buy if you plan to become a professional groomer, since its detachable blade mechanism allows you to switch blades in seconds by sliding the old one off and snapping a new one on. The Model 113, or Lucky Dog Clipper, is recommended for home use only.

1

The correct way to hold the clipper.

Two other clippers should be mentioned briefly, as they can be valuable companion pieces on special occasions:

The Oster Animal Trimmer. A smaller machine than the A-5 or A-2 clippers, with smaller and narrower blades. Because it is small and light in weight, this trimmer is easy to use and handle around sensitive areas. It's an excellent choice for trimming the face, feet, and hard-to-get spots on small Poodles and puppies.

The Andis Cordless Rechargeable Trimmer. This model comes with a stand that automatically recharges the trimmer when it is plugged into a 110 Volt AC outlet. It is an excellent choice for last-minute touch-ups at dog shows.

Photograph 1 shows the best position for holding the clippers, almost as you would hold a pencil. When in use, the blade is always placed flat against the area it clips. *Never point the teeth of the blade into the dog's skin!*

Like any other electric tool or appliance, systematic maintenance will help keep your clipper in good working condition. Whichever model you choose, do remember to study the instruction card that comes along with the clipper.

Maintenance of Oster Clippers:

A new clipper comes out of its box properly oiled and ready to use. Add oil only if the motor develops a squeal caused by a dry bearing. Add one drop of oil to the boiler in the housing. Always use the brand of oil recommended by the clipper manufacturers. This will be a lubricating oil. Certain other oils are penetrating oils. The difference is that a lubricating oil acts as a lubricant to diminish friction while a penetrating oil contains mostly solvent to dissolve rust and does not lubricate.

Just like a new car, a new dog clipper needs a few weeks to become broken in. Don't worry about sluggish performance. It will tend to run hotter and slower until the break-in period is over. Once a month, remove the metal name plate held on by two screws and check the amount of grease inside the cavity. If you need to add grease, remove the lever, link, and gear from the gear post. Clean these parts with a cloth and set them aside. Check the inside of the cavity and remove any old grease that has become clogged with hair. Then insert the tip of the grease tube into the hold on top of the gear post. Squeeze until grease appears out of the top and bottom holes on the side of the post. Do not fill the entire cavity; too much grease will only make the clipper run hotter and slower. Replace the gear, link, and lever, then add a bit of grease to the gear teeth and linkage. Replace the name plate and the job is complete.

Remember, too, that carbon brushes do wear out and need to be replaced. If you don't replace brushes in time, the armature may become damaged, resulting in an expensive repair job. A spare set of brushes comes with each new clipper. Periodically, remove the brush caps and examine the brushes. A little spring fits on the round end of the brush. If the square section is worn to the same length as the round section, then your brushes need to be replaced. Always replace the brushes in pairs, never one at a time. Turn the brushes so that the curve in the square end fits the armature curve.

In normal use, clippers do heat up occasionally. You may be able to avoid overheating, however, by checking the following:

Break-in period: This is a temporary situation previously mentioned.

Proper voltage supply: Check to see that you are plugging your clipper into the proper voltage supply. If you are not (perhaps because of a faulty wiring system, or because you are operating different items on double sockets), your clipper will be undervoltaged. In this situation, a clipper runs slowly, heats up, has slower blade strokes, and does not cut as efficiently.

Hair in clipper: Check the ventilation openings in the end cap. If they are clogged with hair, unscrew the cap (unplug the cord when you do this) and remove the excess hair with a brush or vacuum. Replace the cap to its correct position.

CLIPPER BLADES

Various clipper blades are available which cut the Poodle's hair to different lengths. They are described in the chart on the facing page.

It should be remembered that a blade cuts closer when used against the hair growth than when used with the hair growth. In other words, a #10 blade used against the growth of hair (from the Poodle's tail to its head) would equal the same results as a #15 blade clipped with the growth of hair (from the head to the tail). Similarly, a #15 blade used against the growth looks the same as a #30 blade clipped with the growth of hair.

If new blades do not seem to cut efficiently, possibly the factory-applied preservative used to keep them from rusting has congealed. You can remove this by cleaning the blades with kerosene, then re-oiling them before starting to clip.

Apply a few drops of oil to the mating faces of the cutting blades and tension spring guide before you begin clipping. It is most important that blades be kept well-lubricated. Good lubrication reduces wear on the metal surfaces of the cutting blade which will enable you to retain that "sharp edge" longer. As you are clipping your dog, use some type of spray lube occasionally. These are products which are sprayed directly onto the blade. The primary benefit will be to cool the cutting blades and help keep hair from accumulating between the upper and lower blade.

For best performance, the upper and lower blades must ride together with no foreign matter between the teeth. If, during the clipping operation, your blade starts to pull or streak, hair may have accumulated between the upper and lower blades. To remedy this, pour Oster *Blade Kleen* or a mixture of one part oil and two parts kerosene in a shallow tray to a depth of about 1½ inches. Immerse the blade into the solution with the motor running. Keep the blade immersed for 20 seconds, wipe dry, re-oil, and continue cutting. Once this has been accomplished, if you find your blade is still not cutting properly, hair still may be trapped between the blades. Remove the upper blade by sliding it across the lower blade, then drop both parts in the oil/kerosene mixture for a few seconds. Wipe dry, making sure that all excess hairs have been removed. Slide the upper blade back into position, re-oil, and continue clipping. When separating the upper blade from the lower, always slide them apart rather than disturb the tension which is properly adjusted at the factory.

At the end of each clipping session, all blades should be cleaned and wrapped in the brown oiled paper in which they were originally packaged. If that's not available, use heavy brown paper and oil it lightly. Clipper blades should always be sharpened and conditioned by a professional.

CLIPPER BLADE CHART

CUTTING ACTION	OSTER MODEL A-5	OSTER MODEL A-2	OSTER MODEL 113/"LUCKY DOG"
Plucking length. Leaves hair 5/8″ to 3/4″ long. Excellent for all-over clipping.	#4	#4	Not available
Plucking length. Leaves hair about 1/2″ long. Excellent for all-over clipping.	#5	#5	Skip Tooth
Semi-plucking length. Leaves hair about 1/4″ long.	#7	#7	Coarse
All-purpose length. Leaves hair about 1/8″ long.	#8½	#8½	Not available
Medium length. Shows natural color of the coat. For general and underbody clipping and sensitive dogs.	#10	#10	Medium
Medium/close length. Shows more skin than #10. Use on feet and face of most Poodles.	#15	#15	Fine
Close cutting. Mostly used for show clipping. Beginners should not use this blade unless dog can be clipped closely.	#30	#30	Not available
Extra-fine cutting. Use for show clips and for cleaning surgical areas.	#40	#40	Not available
Close cutting. Blade is 5/8″ wide, smaller than standard size. Good for hard-to-get spots on Toy Poodles.	#5/8	#5/8	#5/8
Close cutting. Blade is 7/8″ wide, smaller than standard size. Good for hard-to-get spots on Toy and Miniature Poodles.	#7/8	#7/8	Not available
Close cutting. Blade is one inch wide. Good for hard-to-get spots and center strip of Dutch Clip on Miniature Poodles.	#8/8	#8/8	Not available
Extra-wide plucking length. Blade is 3/4″ wider than standard size. Leaves hair about 1/2″ long.	Extra Wide Skip Tooth	Extra Wide Skip Tooth	Not available
Extra-wide all purpose length. Blade is 3/4″ wider than standard size. Clips same as #10 blade.	Extra Wide Regular	Extra Wide Regular	Not available

You can also buy various brands of plastic blades that snap onto the regular clipper blade and adjust to most clippers. Generally, these are coarse-cutting and leave the hair from 1/4″ to one inch long.

Purchase the finest barber shears available and keep them sharp and loose. Ideally, you should own two types of shears, a pair with long, straight blades tapering to a point (**D**), and a pair with blunt or round ends (**E**). Blunt-tipped scissors are especially useful for scissoring around the feet, between the pads on the underside of the feet, the topknot, bracelets and tail pompon. They are also recommended for work with nervous dogs or young puppies. Scissors are purchased by length. The length you select depends on the variety you will be grooming as well as on personal preference. Some groomers prefer shorter, lightweight shears in 6½", 7" or 7½" and find longer, heavier scissors to be uncomfortable in their hands. Others like 8", 8½" and 10" shears for all-purpose scissoring. Whatever their size, scissors are all constructed the same, having three basic parts: the bow, the shank, and the blades. The bow forms the handle; the shank is the middle section where the parts join together, and the blades are the working edges.

How to Hold the Scissors

Efficient scissoring can be accomplished when the shears are held correctly, as shown in **Photograph 2.** The thumb slips through the larger of the two openings and the third finger goes through the smaller opening. The little finger rests in the open shank at the bottom of the smaller opening. The index finger rests on the shank for extra support. While this position is the correct way to hold the scissors, some groomers prefer to scissor by placing their middle (instead of the third) finger through the smaller opening, as shown in **Photograph 3.** Either position is acceptable, although the first should be less tiring and more efficient. The ultimate criteria, however, is how the dog looks when finished and how efficiently you accomplished that finished look. In use, best results are obtained when the scissor blades are held flat against the hair. By holding the cutting edge parallel to the ends of the hair, the shaft is cut as wide as the root and creates a thick, profuse look. Try not to hold the scissors at an angle, as this tends to narrow and weaken the ends of the hair.

Suggestions for Use and Maintenance

Scissoring a dirty dog will dull your blades quickly. Try to shampoo and dry the Poodle's hair before using your best scissors. If you do rough-cut before shampooing, use old scissors.

When the scissor blade is sharp, the hair drops off immediately as the scissor closes. When blades begin to

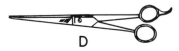

2

The correct way to handle the shears.

3

Another position for holding the shears.

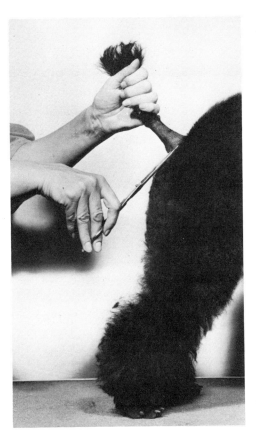

When in use, the scissors should be held flat against the hair.

dull, you will notice that the hair does not drop off immediately as the shear closes, but slips forward towards the pointed ends. When this happens, your shears need sharpening and conditioning by a professional. If you hold scissors in a closed position up to light, you should notice a slight space between the blades. If this were not present, the scissor would not cut properly. If the space is too large, scissoring will be difficult, however, and your scissors should be re-ground and readjusted.

Scissors are made of carbon or stainless steel. The difference between the two is that stainless steel won't rust. Although many people believe that stainless shears do not hold an edge as long as those made of carbon steel, this is not true if you select the finest grade of stainless.

Scissor blades may be plain or serrated. Some groomers prefer serrated blades because they grab the hair shaft and hold it more securely. Scissors with serrated blades will not cut as smoothly, however, as a plain ground shear. They will cut longer, but the finish will be "rougher."

At the end of each day's use, wipe your scissors dry before you put them away. Put several drops of lubricating oil on a tissue and wipe over the blades and edge. Try not to leave fingermarks on the blades, as oil and salt from your hand perspiration can mark carbon steel. Once the scissors are clean, place them in their sheath and store them in a dry place. It's not a good idea to seal scissors in a drawer as moisture can accumulate inside, especially if you live in a humid climate. Badly rusted scissors should be cleaned, repolished and refinished and cared for in the manner previously described. Rust spots can be removed with Naval Jelly which can be purchased in any hardware store.

BRUSHES

The correct brush for a pet Poodle is a slicker, an oblong-shaped (**F**) brush with a wooden handle. Its bent wire teeth are set close together to help remove mats and dead hair. Slicker brushes come in three sizes: small for Toy Poodles, medium for Miniature Poodles, and large for Standard Poodles. Slickers are not recommended for the long mane coat of show Poodles, as the bent wire teeth have a tendency to pull out long hair. However, the new fine-wire slickers can be used to brush out bracelets or packs on show coats.

For show grooming, choose a brush with long, pliable pins or bristles (**G**) set in a cushioned rubber base. The finest pin brushes have long, polished stainless steel or chrome-plated pins with rounded ends to prevent scrat-

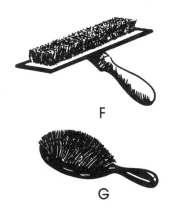

F

G

ching and skin irritation. When passing through the long hair, the pins should be flexible enough not to pull out coat. (Caution: pins that have bent or have sunk into the rubber cushion tend to ruin the coat. When either condition is present, the brush should be replaced.) The finest bristle brushes are those with tufts of natural bristles set in a cushioned rubber base. The bristles in each tuft should be graduated in length to give even and deep penetration through the Poodle's coat.

H

I

COMBS

There are many different types of Poodle combs and, generally, each type is available in fine (for soft coats), medium (for average coat textures), and coarse (for dense coats) teeth spacing. For Standards, use a comb with long round teeth about 2 inches long (**H**) to get deep into the coat. For Miniatures and Toys, use a comb with teeth about one inch long. The most popular professional comb seems to be one with half-fine and half-medium teeth, shown in (**I**). Quality is important; always buy the finest comb you can afford. The best models are made of chrome-plated solid brass and have spring-tempered teeth with rounded tips to prevent scratching and skin irritation.

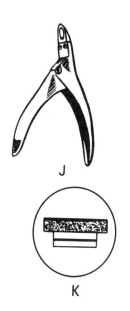

J

K

NAIL CLIPPERS

A variety of nail trimmers are available. They are:

Guillotine type: An implement (**J**) that is held in the palm of your hand. The dog's nail is inserted into the opening above the cutting blade. When the handles are squeezed together, a blade passes over the opening and cuts off a portion of the dog's nail—hence the name "guillotine."

Nail Scissors: These look just like a small pair of scissors. The dog's nail is inserted into the opening and the scissor is pressed together.

Safety Nail Trimmer: A specialty designed tool with a safety stop that can be swung into place to limit the amount of nail to be trimmed.

Clipper Attachments: There are several band or disc type attachments which can be used on the A-2 clipper (**K**). These are mounted onto the clipper when the cutter head is detached.

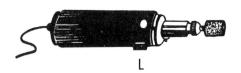

L

Electric Nail Groomers: Many professionals use an electric tool to trim the nails by high rotational speed. These are small tools, about 8 inches long. They have a grinding drum with an abrasive band at one end (**L**). Electric nail sanders grind the nails at excessively high speeds, usually around 25,000 to 30,000 R.P.M. Replacement drums and bands may be purchased separately.

M

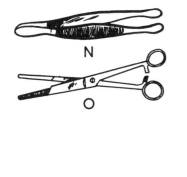

N

O

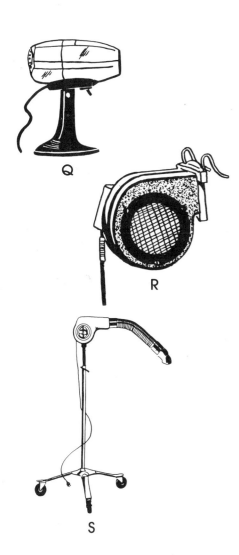

Q

R

S

NAIL FILE

A nail file (**M**) or emery board is necessary to shorten the nails or to smooth the sharp edges left after cutting the nails with a manual trimmer. For best results, draw the file in one direction only, from the top of the nail downward.

TWEEZERS or FORCEPS

Cleaning your Poodle's ears is an important part of grooming. You need a tweezers (**N**) or straight 5″ Kelly Forceps (**O**) to do this job.

DENTAL SCALER

To remove tartar from the teeth, select a right-and-left-angled Dental Scaler (**P**), with a flat, not pointed, surface. Most pet groomers prefer to have a veterinarian scale the dog's teeth.

HAIR DRYER

Electric hair dryers not only speed drying time but also help to achieve a more finished look to the final grooming of the Poodle. For home use, there are many inexpensive small dryers for humans that will dry a Poodle quickly and make his coat fluffy. **Illustration Q** shows one type with a stand, allowing the dryer to be held in the groomer's hand or placed on the grooming table and tilted to any angle to concentrate drying power.

For professional groomers, heavy-duty dryers are designed for use in kennels and grooming salons. A cage dryer (**R**) attaches to a dog crate by brackets. The most popular professional Poodle dryer is the floor or stand model (**S**). Its strong air output can dry the heaviest coat in a short time. The dryer is supported by a sturdy, adjustable-height stand. The legs usually are equipped with ball casters so the dryer can be moved about without difficulty. The dryer has a rubber nozzle that rotates a full 360° to direct air flow where you want it. Of course, heat and air output vary, depending on the model you choose. Some dryers have three-position switches—cold, warm and hot—while others have infinite range heat control, allowing you to select any temperature between cool and hot. Most professional dryers are equipped with thermostats to prevent overheating.

GROOMING TABLE

It is important to use the proper table for grooming, for both the poodle and the groomer should be relaxed and comfortable during the session. The dog should associate being on a grooming table as a pleasant experience. Psychologically, regular grooming sessions should develop into much more than making a dog look presentable or main-

T

taining his coat between shows or professional appointments. They should eventually develop a better understanding between dog and owner—a sort of mutual confidence in one another that grows with the passing of time.

Most groomers and dog exhibitors prefer a firm and sturdy table with a non-slip rubber top. Several types of tables are made for small animal grooming, some of which are portable (T), with rectangular tops in sizes 30 inches long by 18 inches wide, 36 inches long by 24 inches wide, or 48 inches long by 24 inches wide. Portable grooming tables fold up and can be stored away when not in use or conveniently transported to and from dog shows in your car. They usually are about 30 inches high, with tubular chrome-steel legs which are not adjustable. You can, however, buy a portable table with legs that adjust manually from 25 to 40 inches.

Most professional groomers use hydraulic tables with rectangular or oval table tops situated on heavy, tip-proof bases. Some have electrically operated food pedals; others have pedals which operate by pumping the foot. The foot pedals raise, lower, lock and release to allow the tables to revolve 360°. The tables usually adjust from 30 to 39 inches, and some have 1/2 inch graduated pump-raising increments, to allow greater range of variable heights for more comfortable grooming. In addition to all these conveniences, hydraulic tables are extremely solid and do not wobble at any adjusted height.

U

Grooming Slings

Grooming slings (U) are made of canvas and come in small, medium and large sizes for the three Poodle varieties. The sling is attached to a tackle and pulley on a wall bracket which can be put over the grooming table. Amateur and professional groomers often use slings for clipping the feet, face and tail, and brushing out the legs of fussy Poodles.

Grooming Post and Loop

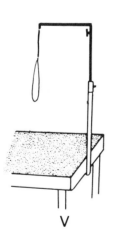

V

A post (V) constructed of heavy gauge chrome steel tubing which can be either bolted to the table top or clamped on the side of the table, depending on the model you choose. At the end of the post is a loop (usually made of nylon or supple leather) that goes round the dog's neck to make him stand in place and prevent him from jumping off the table.

It's not necessary to buy all the equipment mentioned in this chapter. To clip a Poodle, you need a clipper, a few extra blades, a brush and comb, and two pair of good quality scissors—one with pointed ends and the other pair with rounded tips. Add the remaining tools as you progress with your grooming.

Coat Care

BRUSHING AND COMBING THE PET POODLE

The easiest way to keep your Poodle in good condition is to brush and comb the coat regularly. Brushing a Poodle's hair regularly achieves the following results:

It stimulates the growth of new hair.

It removes dead hair before it has a chance to mat near the skin.

It helps keep the skin clean and makes the dog less susceptible to disease and external parasites.

It spreads the natural oils evenly through the coat.

It looks healthier and more glossy than unbrushed hair.

As soon as you acquire a Poodle, you must set up a regular brushing and combing schedule. Three times a week is sufficient providing you brush correctly. The mistake most pet owners make is not brushing the hair to the skin. This means parting the coat and holding down the unbrushed hair with your free hand to separate it from the hair that is being brushed. If you can learn to do this correctly, your dog will never become matted.

Along with the correct brush and comb, you will need a "Coat Conditioner," a specially formulated product that is sprayed lightly onto the hair before brushing. It makes brushing easier, helps remove tangles, eliminates dryness, and adds a shine to the hair which deepens and enriches the natural coat color. Products that contain protein such as Ring 5 Protein Coat Conditioner or Lambert Kay's Pro-Groom not only condition but also help repair damaged hair.

Follow this step-by-step procedure:

 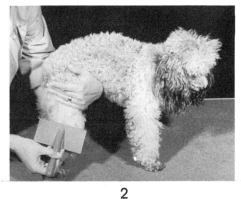 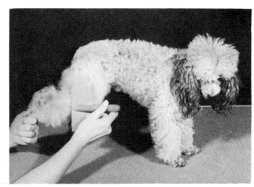

| 1 | 2 | 3 |

Photograph 1 shows an unbrushed poodle.

Photograph 2. While there is no special way to brush a pet Poodle, it seems easier to start at the dog's hindquarters and work forward. Using the slicker brush described in the Equipment Chapter, brush the back legs first, using a downward stroke. Notice that the hair is parted to the skin and that the free hand holds down the unbrushed hair to separate it from the section being brushed.

Photograph 3. Carefully pull the back leg backward and brush the hair upward, using brisk strokes that lift the hair rather than flatten it.

Photograph 4. Continue working forward and brush the tail, hindquarters, back, ribs and chest, parting the hair and brushing to the skin.

Photograph 5. Turn the dog around to stand facing you and brush the front of the chest.

Photograph 6. Gently pull each front leg forward as you brush the hair upward.

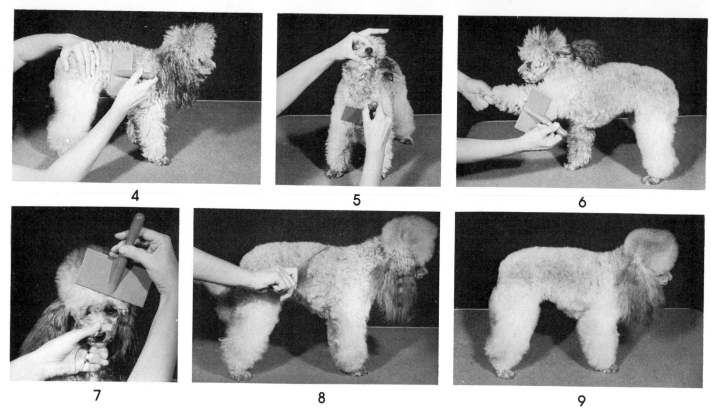

4   5   6

7   8   9

Photograph 7. Place the dog in a sitting position facing you. Brush the topknot upward and backward. Brush the ear feathering downward.

Photograph 8. When the dog is completely brushed, comb through the coat to be sure all tangles are removed.

Photograph 9 shows the Poodle after brushing and combing.

MATTED HAIR

The most common reasons for mats and tangles are neglect in brushing or hair that is incorrectly brushed. While a pet owner may select the correct brush and comb for his or her Poodle, they are often used incorrectly, perhaps only whisking through the top coat, instead of to the skin. Within a short time, a solid block of matted hair forms near the skin.

Even when one knows how to properly brush a Poodle's coat, there are critical "coat matting" periods to face. Long spells of damp weather and humidity make the hair mat easily. Heavy snow is harsh on Poodle hair. Dogs that go outside and become soaking wet tend to mat quickly if the hair is not brushed and dried properly afterwards. The most critical coat period for a Poodle, however, is when the puppy coat is "blowing" or changing into adult texture. At this time, the ends of the hair are rather sparse while the coat at the skin is much thicker as the fine puppy hair is replaced by a coarser hair in the same follicle. During this change-over period, if the Poodle is not brushed daily, the hair mats together almost overnight and forms large clumps near the skin.

Before the groomer can cope with matted hair, it is necessary to understand how tangles form. All types of hair (human and dog) have two basic parts—the root and the shaft. The root is implanted in the skin and the shaft is the part that projects from the surface. The hair shaft is composed of three separate layers: *the cuticle,* or outer layer; *the cortex,* or middle layer, and *the medulla,* or inner layer. The cuticle is formed by overlapping, hard and flat scales called imbrications. These scales protrude upward and outward like barbs in the direction of the hair growth. When there is a lack of oil on the hair shaft, the ragged edges of the barbs lock together (much in the same fashion that a piece of felt is made) and form tangles. If the coat is continually neglected, one solid mat will eventually result. Hair is also charged negatively by static electricity accumulating on the cuticle. Excess electricity causes flyaway ends, but also can cause mats and tangles.

Treating Matted Hair

If the hair is badly matted, you may have to decide whether to cut the dog down or to remove the tangles. With a little patience and practice, though, even the largest mat can be removed with little hair loss. You must, however, consider the comfort of the dog, for no Poodle can be expected to sit quietly while you tear through the coat trying to de-mat it. The easiest and fastest way to save as much coat as possible and to restore the hair to optimum condition is by using a tangle removing product in conjunction with a slicker brush or mat removing tool. Products such as *Ring 5 Untangle* contain untangling components to break the static look and they also contain special conditioning oils to add body, help repair damage caused by tangling, and to help reduce further matting.

For best results, saturate all the matted hair with *Untangle.* Use your fingers to make sure the mats are completely wet. This is important because the combination of lubricants, detanglers and conditioning oils work by lubricating the locked barbs so that one hair slides over the other. Allow the product to remain on the coat until the hair is damp or almost dry. Use your fingers or mat removing tool to pull apart large clumps of mats, separating them into smaller sections. Then brush out each small section. Keep breaking the mats into smaller sections and brushing the hair until the dog is completely tangle-free.

EMERGENCY COAT-SAVING HINTS

To remove beard and moustache stains on white or light-colored Poodles, or to dry clean the coat when the dog is ill or in season: Use a Whitener-Cleaner, such as *Ring 5 Whitener-Cleaner.* Spray on the hair, wait a few minutes, then brush out.

To remove grass or urine stains: Use Whitener-Cleaner. Spray on the hair, wait a few minutes, then brush out.

To remove excessive stains from beard hair: Saturate the stained hair with ginger ale. Let dry, then wash out.

Itching, Scratching, Minor Skin Irritations, Insect Bites, Sunburn, Superficial Cuts or Scratches: Use a medicated spray or a first aid cream. If irritation is severe or problems persists, consult a veterinarian.

Chewing Gum: Rub peanut butter into the gum, let stand a few minutes, then comb out of the coat. Another method is to rub an ice cube over the gum. It will become brittle and pull easily out of the hair.

Grease Spots: Use Fuller's Earth (available at all pharmacies), cornstarch or Whitener-Cleaner. Dust into the coat, wait several minutes, then brush out. Shampoo and rinse thoroughly. Repeat if necessary.

Skunk or Fertilizer Odor: Mix about 5 ounces of Massengill douche powder or liquid (available at most pharmacies) in one gallon of warm water. Saturate the Poodle's hair, taking care not to pour the mixture into the eyes. Do not rinse. Allow the hair to dry, then brush out.

Tar in Coat or Feet: Rub butter or Crisco into the tarred areas and let it remain in the hair until the tar softens and works out of the coat. Shampoo twice and rinse well. Repeat if necessary.

Coat Chewing: Assuming there is nothing physically wrong with the dog and that he may be chewing out of boredom, spray the hair with "Bitter Apple" or dab on a little Tabasco or "Capsicum." The bitter taste should act as a deterrent.

CARE OF THE SHOW COAT

A Poodle must be structurally sound and in top condition if he is to be shown in the breed ring. Physical perfection for a Poodle (actually, for any breed) is achieved by good food, proper exercise, fresh air, and regular grooming over a long period of time. Your first concern must be feeding your Poodle a well-balanced diet, supplemented with the necessary vitamin/mineral supplements. You can't expect results by fussing with the hair without first considering what goes inside to make the coat bloom. Since this is not a book about nutrition, you would benefit greatly by reading *The Collins Guide to Dog Nutrition,* by Donald R. Collins, DVM (also published by Howell Book House). Heed Dr. Collins' advice, feed a well-balanced diet, establish an exercise regimen, and then concentrate on growing the show coat.

If you want to show your Poodle, he must certainly have a good coat texture. The ideal texture as described in the breed standard *"is of naturally harsh texture, dense throughout."* On an adult Poodle with good texture, the coat is so profuse that it seldom parts. The old adage "breeding tells" is positively true for the show prospect. Coat texture is inherited and, without the genes for producing the ideal coat, no Poodle will get it by the spraying on of lotions or potions. Although a Poodle rarely gets his best texture until 18 months of age or older, you need not guess what a puppy's coat will be like when he is an adult. Adult Poodles with good coats start out as puppies with good coats! Your first concern is maintaining the coat by proper brushing.

BRUSHING THE SHOW COAT

Brushing is the most time consuming part of maintaining a show coat because it must be done frequently and there can be no short cuts. As previously mentioned, regular brushing achieves certain desirable results: it stimulates the growth of new hair and makes the coat less inclined to mat. It keeps the skin clean and makes the dog less susceptible to disease and external parasites. The natural oils are distributed more evenly and the individual hairs lie more smoothly. A certain light is reflected from well-brushed hair, making it more glossy than when it is unbrushed.

You need **two different types of brushes** for the show coat: **a pin brush** (with long polished, round-tipped pins) for the mane coat, and **a fine-wire slicker** for the pack and/or bracelets. Along with the right equipment, correct brushing action is necessary. The proper stroke is long and sweeping, going beyond the hair ends to keep them from splitting or snapping off. Very little hair comes out in the brush when you stroke correctly. But you have to practice! The light "rotary" wrist action that lets you brush for hours without tiring or pulling out coat takes patience to perfect.

If you own a puppy, the first step is to teach the prospective show prospect to lie on his side on the grooming table while his coat is being brushed. Some puppies quickly learn to lie still, but others can be frightened and fussy at first. If this happens, don't force your puppy down onto the table. Hold him in your lap instead, maneuvering him on his side, and brush in that position. When the dog learns to relax, move him to the table.

The frequency of brushing a show coat depends on the age, texture and condition of the coat. Each texture varies and responds differently to grooming, as well as products used on the coat. A puppy from four to ten months old usually needs to be brushed three times a week.

However, some time between the ages of 10 and 14 months, the coat begins to change from puppy to adult texture, and the hair almost seems to mat overnight. The top coat looks sparse and straggly, while the undercoat feels much thicker. During this period, you probably will have to brush every day to prevent mats. Changing of the coat texture is exasperating—in fact, it separates the true exhibitor from the amateur, because it's usually the time that many novices decide they are not meant to be Poodle people and cut the dog down. Once this period is complete, however, and the texture totally changed, the adult Poodle coat is rather easy to maintain by brushing three times a week.

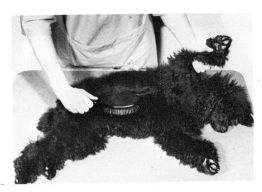

1   2   3

To brush the show coat: Place the dog on his side on the grooming table with feet facing you. The long puppy hair or the mane coat of the English Saddle or Continental Clip, is layer brushed. Begin by parting the hair lengthwise from the shoulder to the rear, as shown in **Photo 1**. Make the part with your fingers, the brush, or a knitting needle. Spray the hair above and below the part with an antistatic coat dressing, such as Coat Gloss, or a light oil, such as Ring 5 Protein Conditioner. Never brush the hair dry; that causes static electricity which can snap off the hair ends, or encourage mats to form. It's not necessary to saturate the coat, just moisten it lightly. You can even spray the mist above the coat and let it float down and settle on the hair.

Place your brush on the part, and brush with a long and sweeping stroke (**Photo 2**). Hold the brush loosely in your hand, almost letting the handle swing like a metronome. Use your free hand to hold down the unbrushed hair to separate it from the section being brushed. Make another part lengthwise about one inch above the hair you have just finished, and "mist" and brush that section the same way. Keep parting the hair in layers as you work up to the center of the back, until one side is finished. To reach the hard-to-get spots under the chest, lift the front leg, as shown in **Photo 3**. Turn the Poodle over and use this same method to spray and brush the other side.

Put the Poodle in a sitting position, facing you, and brush the hair on the front end of the chest downward. If the topknot and ears were not brushed while the dog was lying on his side, do them now. Stand the Poodle on the table and use the fine-wire slicker to brush the tail, and the legs of the Puppy Clip, or the pack and/or bracelets of the show clips. If you want a curly pack on the English Saddle clip, don't brush the hair. Instead, spray it with water or a non-oily coat dressing, then comb it to encourage natural curls to form.

COAT CARE BETWEEN SHOWS

To best condition the puppy coat, use a light oil. One with protein adds body and eliminates flaking, and helps repair damaged hair, rather than just give an attractive sheen for a few days. Such a conditioner should be used during the brushing process at least twice a week. Shampoo the puppy every ten days to two weeks. Once a month, tip off the ends of the coat with scissors, as instructed in the *Puppy Clip chapter. As the topknot and ear feathering grow longer, they should be wrapped to prevent the ends from snapping off, and to encourage growth.*

During the coat change, if the hair mats excessively, you may want to try a more substantial oil to condition, as well as to retard tangling. The aerosol Ring 5 Show Ring, or the heavier Wu-Pi, Rich Health Oil Treatment, or a mixture of one capful of Alpha Keri (available at any pharmacy) to one cup of water, and other such products are ideal at this time. These are applied to the hair as it is layer brushed or, in the case of the heavier oils, after the final rinse of a bath. (After a shampoo, incidentally, don't rinse off the oil. Towel the excess moisture from the coat, then brush and dry.) Shampoo the Poodle every ten days to two weeks at this time and, if he is not going to a show, immediately put him back into oil. Wrap his topknot and ear feathering. Heavy oil sometimes causes the skin to flake excessively. If this happens, you'll have to take the dog out of oil for a while, until the skin becomes normal. After you remove the heavy oil and keep it off for several weeks, pay careful attention to your Poodle's coat. Traces of oil can ooze from the skin for several days after the shampoo. You must brush the coat faithfully at least once a day, and possibly spray a Whitener-Cleaner, or sprinkle silicone grooming powder or cornstarch into the hair to absorb the oil.

When the coat reaches the desired length and the change-over from puppy to adult texture is complete, maintain the adult coat with a protein conditioner or the slightly heavier Show Ring with mink oil. This (and other products with mink oil) contains an ultraviolet sunscreen to protect the coat against sun discoloration. Do remember that oil is used only between shows, and must be completely shampooed from the hair before a dog is exhibited in the breed ring.

As a rule, it's best to bathe a Poodle a few days before a show. Bathing softens the hair, and shampooing three to four days beforehand helps to restore the coat's natural harshness. If the Poodle is white or light-colored, however, you may have to rebathe the pack, bracelets and tail the day before the show to restore that "crisp" appearance. Shampoo with any of the products mentioned in the *Bathing* chapter, and follow with a creme rinse or superconditioner. If the dog is in heavy oil, a detergent may be necessary to remove it from the coat. Use the following if necessary: in an empty gallon jug, pour one quart of Liquid Lux dish detergent. Add four ounces USP glycerine and four ounces of white vinegar. Fill the jug to the top with water. Shake well and shampoo. Use this mixture *only* when the oil cannot be removed with the products mentioned in the *Bathing* chapter.

A

CARE OF THE TOPKNOT

As the Poodle's topknot grows long, the hair should be wrapped in plastic paper ("Baggies," etc.), waxed paper, florist's or tissue paper, or Marcel Interfold Dry Waxed paper (available at certain bakeries). We appreciate that a list of so many materials to choose from may be confusing, but you can experience different results depending on coat texture, climate or humidity. Experiment to find out which material is best for your Poodle.

Cut a strip about six inches long and four inches wide. Sit the dog on the grooming table, facing you. Part the hair across the top of the head from in from in front of one ear to the front of the other ear (**A**). Before wrapping, spray the hair with a light oil, then brush it smooth. Place the

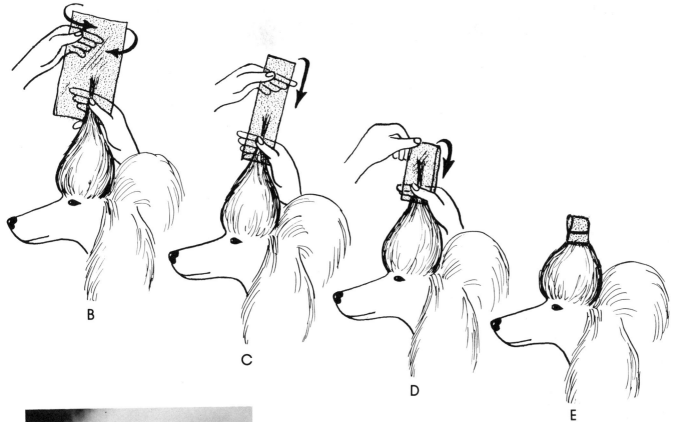

B

C

D

E

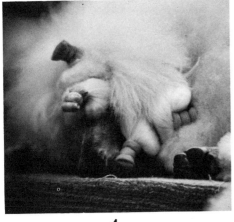

1

1. Poodles with long topknots may require two (or more) wrappers. (Notice, too, that this Poodle has two wrappers on its ears.)

2

wrapping behind the hair (**B**), folding it lengthwise around the topknot. Fold the paper in half (**C**), then in half once again (**D**). Fasten with a latex band (**E**). If wisps of topknot hair slip out of the wrapper, place a strip of cotton around the hair before completing (**B**), gathering all the wispy ends underneath. Additional sections (behind the first) should be wrapped if the topknot is long (**Photo 1**). Remove the wrapper(s) several times a week, spray and brush the hair, then rewrap.

Some Poodles fuss when their topknots are wrapped. They rub their heads on the floor or in their crates, and do other no-nos to pull out the wrappers. If this happens with your Poodle, use another method to protect the topknot. Part the hair across the top of the head as previously instructed. Loop a small latex band around the center of the hair section, close to the skull (but not tight enough to distort the eye), just as you were putting up the topknot. Loop another band around this section of hair, well above the lower one, forming a sort of queue. Make another part across the top of the head behind the first one, then secure this section of hair with latex bands in the same manner. Join the two queues or braids together with separate latex bands. If the topknot is very long, you may have to use quite a few bands (**Photo 2**). When you want to take down this arrangement, cut the bands carefully with scissor points; never pull them out of the dog's hair.

31

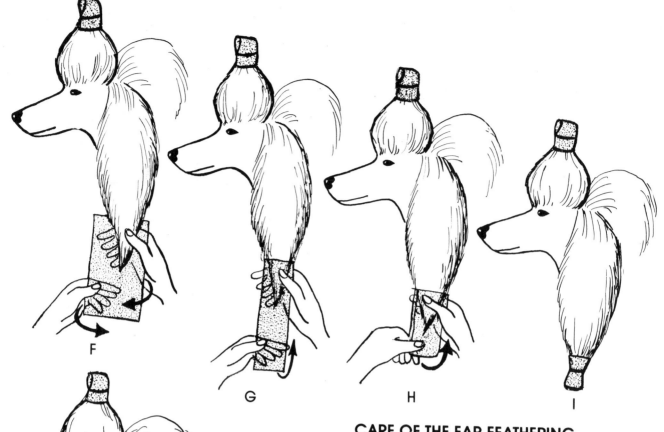

F G H I

J

CARE OF THE EAR FEATHERING

The best way to protect the long ear feathering from being damaged and to encourage it to grow, is to wrap the hair in any of the previously mentioned materials. Cut two wrappers about six inches long and four inches wide. Spray the ear fringes with a light oil, and brush them smooth. Place a wrapper behind the feathering on one ear (**F**), folding it lengthwise. Fold the wrapper in half (**G**), and then in half again (**H**). Fasten with a small latex band. (**I**) Wrap the opposite ear. Be sure to keep the wrappers below the tips of the ear leathers. If you include the ear tip in the wrapper, blood circulation will be interrupted and the ear will be damaged. After both ears are wrapped, take a comb and see if you can place the teeth between each wrapping and ear leather (**J**). Your Poodle may object to all this and try to chew off the wrappers. To discourage him, dab a little Bitter Apple, Capsicum, or Tabasco on them or, as a substitute, eliminate the wrappers completely and loop a latex band around the feathering below each ear leather (**Photo 3**).

Remember:
1. Spray and brush the topknot and ear feathering before wrapping.
2. Do not wrap topknot hair or ear feathering that is wet or dirty.
3. Remove wrappers at least three times a week; brush the hair thoroughly, then re-wrap.

3

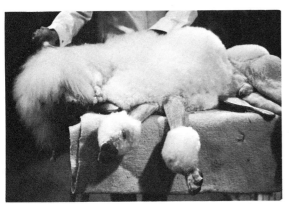

At the dog show... *Left:* A Standard Poodle rests on his side for brushing. *Center:* Before completing final scissoring, place the show lead around the Poodle's neck and temporarily gather the excess together with a rubber band to keep it out of the way. *Right:* Finishing touches are being applied to a Miniature Poodle in English Saddle clip. His mane coat has been brushed, his topknot put up, and a show lead placed around his neck. To complete his grooming, ear wrappers will be removed and the feathering brushed.

GROOMING AT A DOG SHOW

Prepare your tack box the evening before the show including, of course, the tools and supplies you will need to prepare the dog for the ring. These will include a pin and slicker brush, comb, scissors, latex bands, and a *non-oily* coat dressing. (Once the dog is bathed before a show, you don't want to brush the hair with an oily product.)

Plan to arrive at the show well ahead of the scheduled judging time. This lets you set up your grooming table and prepare your dog for the ring in a leisurely manner. If you arrive late and put your dog together at breakneck speed, he may be bewildered by the time he gets into the ring.

Place the dog on his side on the grooming table, and spray his mane coat with a mist of coat dressing. To avoid overwetting, spray the mist above the coat and let it float down and settle onto the hair. Brush the long hair in layers with a pin brush until it dries. Stand the dog on the table and brush the tail, pack, and/or bracelets with a fine-wire slicker. Place the show lead around the Poodle's neck, gathering the excess together temporarily with a rubber band, while you complete the finishing touches.

Remove the topknot wrappers, spray the hair lightly with coat dressing, then brush with a pin brush until it dries. Put up the topknot (*instructions and photographs for doing this are found under the English Saddle Clip*). Comb out the pack and/or bracelets and rescissor any areas that need touching up. Comb the mane coat outward, upward and slightly forward, then comb the topknot upward and outward to blend with the hair around the neck. Rescissor the ruff to tip off any straggly ends that spoil the round outline. If the topknot is too long, shorten the ends with scissors to create a better balance with the mane coat. Ideally, you want to topknot to frame the face and show the head and expression off to advantage.

Remove the ear wrappers, mist the feathering lightly with coat dressing, then brush the hair downward with a pin brush. Once dry, the tips of the hair may be evened with scissors. To keep the hair in place, most handlers and exhibitors like to spray a fine mist of coat dressing or hair spray around the head (covering the Poodle's eyes with a free hand). If you wish to do this before entering the ring, never overspray with heavy lacquers that stiffen or alter the natural texture of the coat.

Bathing, Fluff-Drying and Maintenance

HOW OFTEN YOU SHAMPOO YOUR POODLE depends on his coat texture, color (how quickly he gets dirty), and the temperature and humidity of your area. Most pet Poodles are bathed monthly, but if you use a fine-quality, correctly pH balnced shampoo (see below), you can bathe as often as necessary.

Preparing a Poodle for a bath is as important as the actual shampoo. All tangles must be carefully brushed and combed from the coat beforehand. If they are not, the mats tend to clump together when the hair is wet, making them even more difficult to remove after the shampoo. And when shampoo is used on matted hair, it's difficult to rinse out.

Choosing the Right Shampoo

Choose a fine-quality shampoo that is correctly pH balanced for dogs. The determination of pH is an important factor in animal as well as human hair and skin care. All chemicals are acid, alkali, or neutral. The degree of acidity or alkalinity in a product is measured by a pH scale which runs from 0 to 14, with 7—the half-way point —being neutral. Anything between 0 and 7 is acid; anything between 7 and 14 is alkaline. Human hair and skin are slightly acid. Therefore, "acid balanced" or "non alkaline" shampoos are properly pH balanced for use on human hair. The pH range for the dog's skin and hair is not the same as that of humans, and is slightly more alkaline. Thus, dogs need an alkaline balanced shampoo to keep their coat and skin at the healthiest, strongest state. They should not be bathed regularly with a low pH acid-balanced shampoo.

Within the grouping of correctly pH balanced shampoos for dogs, you can find many products designed for general or special use from such top manufacturers as Ring 5, Lambert Kay, Oster, Rich Health and other companies. Some of these include:

All-purpose shampoos: These are formulated for all coat textures and all colors. Some contain protein, balsam, placenta, panthenol and other conditioners. All-purpose shampoos clean beautifully, add just the right amount of body and keep the coat in optimum condition. Those with special conditioning ingredients help to restore lustre to dull hair and, depending on the added conditioner, to rebuild damaged hair.

Tearless shampoos: These are mild formulations, especially recommended for puppies and Poodles with sensitive skins.

Medicated shampoos: These are formulated to help relieve itching, scaling, bacterial fungus and non-specific types of dermatitis.

Color shampoos: These are formulated for specific coat colors. They are not permanent dyes or color changers, but products which enhance the natural coat color through the use of optical brighteners by highlighting rather than changing. For instance, shampoos for white and light-colored Poodles help to remove yellow or grayish discolorations from the hair. Products for black/blue Poodles or for the brown/apricot range help to remove oxidation (or more simply, the reddish/orangey tipping) and make the coat a more normal color.

Texturizing or body building shampoos: These are formulated to add body and are recommended for soft coats when more texture is desired.

Insecticidal shampoos: These are high-quality, oil-based products formulated to kill fleas and ticks. They clean and condition the coat at the same time and, when used according to directions, are safe for puppies.

Preparing for the Bath

After your Poodle is thoroughly brushed and combed, take him out to relieve himself. Clean any dirty hairs off your grooming table and spread one large, thick bath towel on top. Place a clean brush and comb on the tabletop, and have the hair dryer ready to switch on as soon as you place the wet dog back on the table.

Next, gather together all the equipment and supplies you need for the bath: a rubber mat for the tub bottom; spray hose; shampoo brush; sponge or washcloth; cotton; mineral oil; shampoo; creme rinse or hair conditioner, and several large bathtowels.

Where you bathe your Poodle depends on his size and your grooming area. Small and medium-sized dogs can be bathed easily in one side of a stationary tub. (If you are a breeder/exhibitor or professional groomer, it's less tiring to have a junior-sized bath tub elevated waist high in your grooming room.) Professionals use different methods of bathing Poodles. Some like to fill the tub with about 2 to 3 inches of warm water, then add about 1/2 cup of shampoo, swirl it around to make suds, and then stand the dog in the water. Others prefer to put the dog in the tub, wet him down with the spray hose and let the water run free during the shampoo. Whichever method you choose is a matter of personal preference—either way will get the dog clean. Use warm water throughout the shampoo; cold water tends to make the coat limp and hot water activates overactive sebaceous glands.

Plug the ears with cotton before putting the dog into the tub. If your Poodle has chronic ear trouble, make certain that no water gets into the ears to further irritate them by putting a little vaseline on the end of the cotton that is inserted in the ears. If you are not using a tearless shampoo, place a drop of mineral oil into each eye for protection from the soap. Attach the spray hose to the faucet and place the rubber mat in the bottom of the tub to keep the dog from slipping.

Shampooing the Pet Poodle

Stand the Poodle in the tub. Wet the hair thoroughly except for the head and ears. By working from the back to the front of the dog—if the dog is infested with fleas, shampoo from front to back—and wetting the head and ears last, your Poodle will be less frightened in the water. Speak quietly and reassuringly as you wet him.

Squeeze fresh shampoo on the hair and shampoo the tail, back legs, body, underbody, front legs, shoulders and chest. Don't be afraid to give a brisk shampoo with your fingertips or the shampoo brush/sponge; your Poodle will enjoy it! Pay attention to stubborn spots between the front and back lets and at the hock joints by using extra shampoo and the sponge. Don't forget the area under the tail, using the sponge to clean any dirty spots. Many groomers like to check the anal glands at this point. Once any fluid has been squeezed with cotton, the unpleasant odor is easily washed with the soapy water.

By now, the only part that has not been shampooed is the head and ears, which has been purposely left dry to make the dog less frightened. Wet the head and ears and wash these parts with the sponge or washcloth, taking care not to get shampoo into the eyes. To avoid eye irritation, it's best to use a tearless shampoo on the head.

Rinse the hair lightly and shampoo a second time. It takes two shampoos to really clean Poodle hair. After using the second sudsing, rinse every trace of shampoo out of the coat. Using warm water and the spray attachment, start at the head and ears and work methodically toward the tail and down the legs, *rinsing and rinsing until clear water comes off the Poodle.* If the dog is standing in water, remember to pull the plug and let all the suds drain out before beginning the final rinse. Thorough rinsing is important. When suds are left in, the coat feels gritty, looks dull, and is impossible to scissor finish.

Creme Rinse or Hair Conditioner

You may wish to use a creme rinse or hair conditioner on your Poodle's coat after the shampoo. A creme rinse helps make the hair more manageable and less inclined to mat after bathing. A conditioner, such as *Hair Care,* moisturizes the hair and skin, restructures the hair shaft, restores elasticity, and adds a depth of color. Depending on the brand you select, these products are applied after the final rinse, left on the coat for the required amount of time, and then rinsed out.

Fluff Drying the Pet Poodle

Squeeze the excess water from the Poodle's coat, then let him shake well. Cover him with a towel to soak up moisture, take him out of the tub and stand him on the grooming table. Remove the wet cotton from his ears and use dry cotton to absorb any moisture inside.

Dry the Poodle with an electric hair dryer set on "Warm." Never set your dryer on "Hot," as too much heat at too close a range strips some of the natural oils and moisture from the hair. As you begin drying, the dog will probably shiver because he is damp. The easiest way to keep him warm is to put him on a dry towel and let him curl his leg up under the body. The excess moisture on the legs will be absorbed by the towel while you dry the head, ears, and body. If you brush the Poodle as he dries, the coat will dry faster and be fluffier. Point the dryer nozzle at the area to be brushed, while you use light strokes to lift rather than flatten the hair. Always keep a spray bottle filled with water (some groomers add 1 to 2 tablespoons of creme rinse) or a non-oily dressing, such as Coat Gloss, nearby to respray areas that dry too quickly and become wavy or "frizzy."

Bathing a Poodle in Show Coat

Poodles in show coat should be bathed and fluff dried regularly. A shampoo routine is as important as regular brushing because clean hair grows faster and is healthier than dirty hair.

Brush the Poodle thoroughly before the bath following brushing instructions for show coats. Before putting the dog in the tub, part the long hair down the center of the back with a pin brush, letting the mane coat fall to either side of the body. Bathe in the manner described previously, always taking care to keep the part down the back to prevent the long hair from tangling. When bathing a Poodle in show coat, don't swirl the hair around with your fingers or a brush, but gently squeeze shampoo through the coat, as if you were washing a delicate sweater. When the Poodle is shampooed all over, rinse carefully, and shampoo a second time. If he's being conditioned in heavy oil, three shampoos may be necessary to remove all oil traces from the coat. (If heavy oil is difficult to remove, shampoo with the Lux, glycerin and vinegar mixture mentioned in the Show Coat care section.)

After the final rinse, use a creme rinse or liquid superconditioner such as Hair Care on the coat. Leave the conditioner on for the required length of time, then rinse thoroughly once again. Squeeze the excess moisture from the coat carefully and blot it with a towel.

Drying the Show Coat

Drying the show coat takes time, and must be done with no short cuts or you can ruin the hair. Place the dog on the grooming table, lying on his side. The wet part nearest the table top should rest on a large and thick bath towel to keep the coat from drying too quickly or tangling.

If the Poodle is in the English Saddle or Continental trim, dry the pack and/or bracelets first, brushing upward with a slicker to create a dense and profuse look. (If you're planning to have a curly pack on the English Saddle, don't fluff dry this area with the brush. Instead, just lift it with the comb to encourage curls to form, then let it dry naturally.)

As you dry the mane coat, part the hair in layers (*see illustrations in the show coat brushing section*) and brush lightly with a pin brush. Begin near the center of the back and make a part from neck backwards to the hindquarters. When this section is brushed and dried to the skin, make another lengthwise part about an inch lower, and brush and dry that section. Use a gentle, sweeping brush stroke that goes beyond the ends of the hair to keep the tips from splitting or breaking. Layer and dry the hair in this manner until you reach the elbow. Lift the front leg and dry as much of the brisket and chest as you can. Dry the ear and the part of the neck and topknot on that side. Always keep your dryer set on "Warm," not "Hot." Keep in mind that during the drying process you are pulling and stretching the wet hair. Hair has a great amount of elasticity, but it can be overstretched, weakened and damaged by hot air. Always keep a spray bottle filled with non-oily coat dressing or water (some groomers add 1 to 2 tablespoons of creme rinse) nearby to respray areas that are drying too quickly.

When one side is completely dry, pick up the dog, remove the wet towel from the table top, put down a dry towel, and turn the dog over. Brush and dry the other side using the same layering method. Before turning off the dryer, feel the hair and skin to make sure there are no damp areas, especially on the ears, the neck, shoulders or chest. These can become curly, or possibly turn into matted clumps overnight if the Poodle's coat is changing from puppy to adult texture. Wrap the ears and topknot when the hair is dry.

TRIMMING THE POODLE'S NAILS

Trimming the nails is an important part of the Poodle's grooming routine, but one that owners often neglect. Most dogs detest having their nails clipped, so they should be trained during puppyhood (especially show prospects) to learn to accept this part of grooming. When the nails are trimmed regularly, they stay short and neat. When the nails are neglected, they keep growing long and eventually make the feet spread and cause serious damage to the dog's legs and feet. Walking and running become uncomfortable, even painful, and eventually, the dog may become lame. Infrequent sessions often result in a battle between you and the Poodle when you do try to shorten the nails. Such sessions are potentially critical for show prospects, for they may cause a dog to associate the handling of his feet as a negative experience and later, he may shy away from the judge's examination of these parts in the ring.

Long nails may not always be the result of deliberate neglect. It's surprising how many people believe that dogs naturally wear down their nails. While this may be true of wild animals, things are a little different with their domesticated cousins. Dogs that walk or exercise regularly on city pavements, concrete runs or hard ground may wear down their nails naturally, but they are in the minority. The average dog spends most of his time indoors and when he does go outside, usually it's to a grassy lawn or other surface too soft to shorten the nails. Therefore, you must establish a regular schedule for nail trimming. Use either of the following methods to shorten the nails:

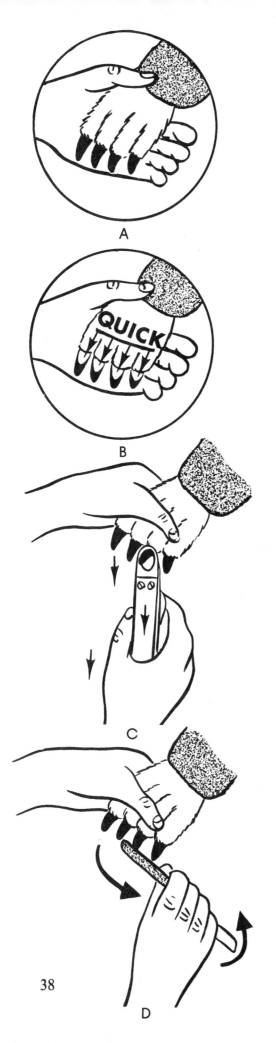

A

B

C

D

Method A—MANUAL NAIL TRIMMER and FILE

Sit the dog facing you on a grooming table or other sturdy surface. It is important that you have proper control over the dog. Hold one of the feet in the palm of your hand (**A**), and pull it gently forward. If the dog fusses or shakes or moves his foot during the trimming, have someone steady him by placing a hand at the elbow as you cut the nails on each front foot, and at his hock joint as you cut the nails on each back foot.

Insert the tip of the nail into the timmer opening (**B** and **C**) and cut it back a little at a time. The outside of each nail is composed of a hard protein called keratin. Inside the nail is a soft, fleshy area called the "quick," which contains the nerves and blood supply. Usually, the quick is easily seen inside the nails of white and light-colored Poodles, but it's almost impossible to locate on dark-colored dogs. The quick is very sensitive and tender and cutting into it will sever the capillaries and cause bleeding.

If you do cut into the quick and cause bleeding, press a little Monsels Powder or nail clotting solution (available from pet supply dealers or dog show concessionaires) against the nail for a few seconds to stop it. Cut each nail back in this manner. If your Poodle has a dewclaw or extra toe on the inside of each front leg just above the foot, its attached nail should be trimmed like the others.

After the nails are cut back, smooth away any rough edges with a nail file or emery board. Draw the file in one direction, from the top of each nail downward, in a curved stroke to the end of the nail (**D**).

Method B—ELECTRONIC NAIL GROOMER or SANDING DISC FOR A-2 CLIPPER

It takes a little practice to become accustomed to using an electric nail groomer or sanding disc, but once you master the proper technique, sanding is a fast way to shorten the nails, with no rough edges.

If your Poodle is fussy, *have someone steady him until he becomes familiar with the sound of the motor.* Place your dog in either of two positions: (**1**) Sitting facing you on a grooming table or other sturdy surface. In this position, you will hold the foot you intend to work on in the palm of your hand (**E**) pulling it gently forward, as previously instructed for manual trimmers; or (**2**) standing on the grooming table while you work from behind or beside each foot. In this position, the nails on each back foot are sanded with the leg pulled backwards. The nails on each

E

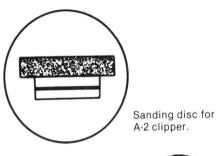

Sanding disc for
A-2 clipper.

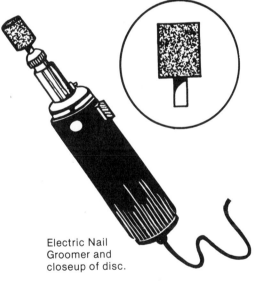

Electric Nail
Groomer and
closeup of disc.

front foot are sanded by gently bending the leg at the carpal joint. The second position is recommended for Standards, and particularly for "fussers," because they can't easily see or interfere with the sander in operation.

Once the dog is in position, turn on the electric groomer and place the grinding disc against the side of a nail, rolling it gently to the center. Repeat the same procedure on the other side of the nail. Sand in short strokes, and *don't press on the nail very long because it gets extremely hot.* One feature of an electric trimmer that most people don't recognize is the extreme heat build up, caused by the friction of the disc on the nail. The heat can cause more pain to a dog than cutting into a quick.

Be careful to hold the sander near the nails and not close to the leg hair while the motor is running, otherwise the hair may catch and wind around the disc as it rotates. Another caution—*and a serious one*—is the long ear feathering. Should the dog lower his head to see what you are doing while the motor is running, the long hair could become tangled in the rapidly rotating disc and cause excruciating pain. To prevent this from happening to a curious Poodle, temporarily tie up his ear feathering with a latex band while the sanding is in progress.

Sand each nail back to the quick. By working in short strokes on each side of the nail, you should spot the quick easily before you reach it. It is possible to sand too far back and make the nail bleed. Usually, this kind of bleeding is not the profuse spurt that comes when the quick is severed by a manual trimmer. Monsels Powder or nail clotting solution will stop the bleeding quickly.

Another point to remember is that the quick recedes when the nails are cut or sanded regularly. When they are neglected, the quick grows long too, and it's almost impossible to shorten the nails without severing the quick.

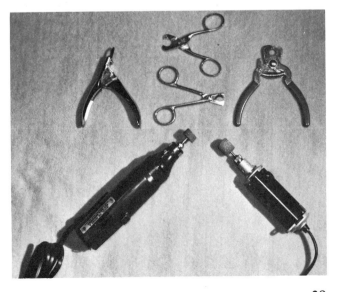

Tools for nail trimming. Pictured at top (l. to r.): Manual Trimmers, guillotine, scissor, and safety types. Below, electric nail sanders.

CARE OF THE POODLE'S EARS

CLEANING THE EARS is another important part of your Poodle's grooming routine. If they are attended to every month, the ears should remain in good condition and the cleaning will take only a short time. The most common reason for neglecting the Poodle's ears is lack of understanding of the ear canal by the novice groomer.

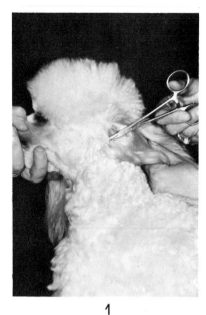

1

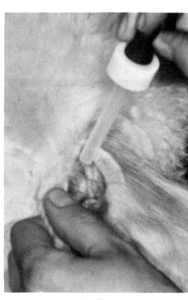

2

The first step in cleaning the ears is to remove the long hair leading into the canal. If this hair is neglected and allowed to grow long, wax will accumulate inside, cut off the air circulation and eventually cause infection. Always do this job on a sturdy grooming table with adequate lighting. Sit the dog on the table. Turn back the ear flap. Use your thumb and index finger or a Kelly 5½ inch fine-point forceps (**Photograph 1**) to carefully pull out the excess hair leading into the canal. (If you are a beginner, only use your fingers to pull out the hair. Never probe inside the ear with an instrument. You could puncture the eardrum if you don't know what you are doing.) Never probe deeper than you can actually see, and remove a few hairs at a time, otherwise it will hurt the dog. If the hair is difficult to grip, shake a little ear powder into the opening to give you a better hold.

Once the hair is removed, moisten a cotton ball with alcohol or a canine ear cleaning lotion, and carefully wipe around the ear flap and the opening into the canal. Don't probe deeply in the canal. If there is no evidence of wax accumulation or a foul smell, your job is finished.

If there is a great deal of wax on the cotton, you will have to flush out the canal. Grasp the cartilage at the base of the ear (**Photograph 2**), and gently pull it out and away from the Poodle's head. Put several drops of ear lotion (formulated to loosen excess wax) into the canal. When the ear is held open in this manner, any medication placed inside will promote proper cleaning. Steady the head with your hand to keep the dog from shaking as you massage the base of the ear with the other hand to spread the lotion inside. After a short massage, let go of the muzzle. Your Poodle will shake his head, but don't be concerned. This is nature's way of protecting the ear canal and bringing the wax to the surface. Once the wax floats up to the surface, remove it with clean cotton balls until the ear is dry.

Poodles that are prone to severe and chronic ear infections and accumulate excessive amounts of wax deep inside the ear should be attended to by a veterinarian. If you notice your dog shaking his head persistently, scratching his ears, carrying one ear lower than the other, or if the ears have a foul odor and a reddish-brown discharge, seek professional attention immediately.

CARE OF THE EYES

YOUR POODLE'S EYES should be checked daily and cleaned of any foreign matter that has collected on the inside corners. The best way to do this is to saturate a cotton ball with warm water, raise the dog's head, gently open the lower lid, and allow the water to drop into the eye. Then use cotton to absorb the excess moisture that floats to the eye corners. Never rub over the eyeball with cotton because you may scratch it and cause irritation.

White and light-colored Poodles, especially Toys, sometimes have dark-stained hair under the eyes caused by a discharge from the tear ducts. The discharge often makes the hair an unsightly reddish-brown, often creating the effect of dark circles under the eyes. Excessive tearing is caused by many reasons: heredity, allergy, neglect in grooming the face, infection of the tear ducts, improper diet, conjunctivitis or teething. Your veterinarian may be able to determine the cause of excessive tearing and control it.

Daily attention to the eye area can help to keep staining at a minimum. First, comb the hair under the eyes with a fine-tooth comb to clean away accumulated matter. Next, a soothing eye lotion (designed to clean the eye of dirt and foreign particles that may enhance tearing) should be applied.

  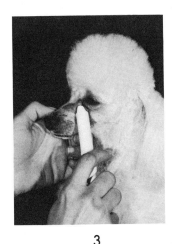 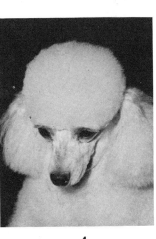

1   2   3   4

For extreme cases of eye stain, the following steps may help to camouflage the discolorations temporarily:

Photograph 1. An unclipped white Toy Poodle. Notice the excessive stains on the hair under the eyes.

Photograph 2. Before camouflaging. The Poodle has been brushed, bathed and dried, and the face clipped. The deep stains are as obvious and ugly as before.

Photograph 3. After clipping, a stick is pencilled under each eye and blended with fingers until the stain disappears. Specially formulated products, such as Safari's Liner Stick, are available in several colors to blend into the natural coat. The Liner Stick helps to retard further staining. If such products are not available from your pet supplies dealer or show concessionaire, you can try several alternatives: a "concealer" makeup for humans, "Clown White" makeup, or Desitin ointment (the last is available at pharmacies). *These products, including Liner Sticks, are only for use on the hair under the eyes and not in a dog's eyes.*

Photograph 4. The stains are completely covered and the dog's appearance improved. Eye stain is a recurring problem, however, and the dog that has it will experience it again unless regular eye care is observed.

CARE OF THE POODLE'S TEETH

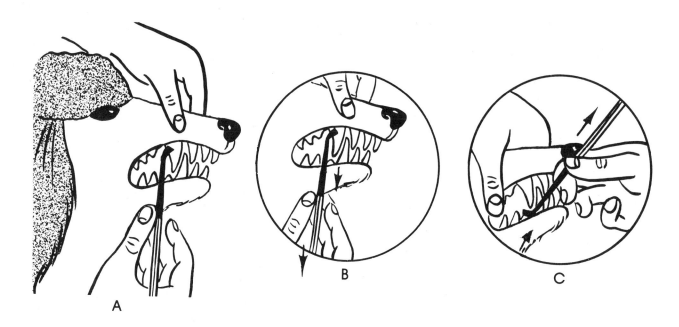

A   B   C

POODLES have two sets of teeth, the baby or "milk" teeth and the permanent teeth. Baby teeth appear when a puppy is three weeks old. They begin falling out and are replaced by permanent teeth when the dog is about 16 weeks old. Teething usually takes from two to four months. Most dogs go through the teething period comfortably, but others suffer from sore gums and high fever and must be treated gently. Occasionally, permanent teeth appear before the baby teeth fall out and the dog may have two teeth in the same spot. If this happens, and you intend to show your Poodle, ask your veterinarian to remove the baby tooth so the permanent bite will not be spoiled.

Periodically, the teeth should be cleaned by rubbing them with a moist cloth that has been dipped into a mixture of equal parts baking soda and salt. Never clean your dog's teeth with a toothbrush. A loose bristle could lodge in the gums between the teeth and cause the dog great pain.

Just like a human being, softness or brittleness in a dog's teeth is hereditary. Many dogs have soft and defective teeth even though they have been fed a well balanced diet. Soft teeth tend to quickly accumulate tartar around the gum line. To keep the teeth and gums free from infection, this tartar must be scraped off. This is not a pleasant job to do since no dog enjoys having his teeth scraped. Many people prefer to let the veterinarian remove tartar.

If you wish to do this job at home, you will need a dental scaler with right and left angles as illustrated in the Equipment Chapter. If a dental scaler is not available at your local pet shop, ask your dentist to order one for you.

Place your dog on a study grooming table. Study the illustrations at the top of this page. Begin by scraping the tartar from the top teeth. Place the sharp part of your scaler up under the gum line (see correct position in **A**). Then scrape downward, using your free thumb to shield the gums and lips below (**B**). Tartar seldom accumulates on the bottom teeth, but if it is necessary to scrape these teeth, place the edge of the scaler under the gum line (**C**) and scrape upward, using your thumb to shield the upper teeth. Pushing the scaler under the gum line and scraping the teeth usually makes the gums bleed. After the tartar is removed, moisten a cotton swab with colorless merthiolate and paint the gums to prevent infection. Disinfect your scaler before and after you use it.

CARE OF THE ANAL GLANDS

EVERY DOG has a pair of anal glands located on the sides of and just below the opening to the anus. These glands secrete a brownish-yellow fluid which empties into the anus. The exact function of the anal glands is often disputed. Some experts believe that they secrete a lubricant to help the dog move its bowels easily. Others believe that the anal glands are vestigial musk glands left over from the dog's primitive state, which once functioned like those of a skunk to frighten away possible attackers. It is true that the skunk's musk glands are located in the same spot as the dog's anal glands, and the secretion from the skunk's glands is similar to that of the dog except for the intensity of odor.

Sometimes the anal glands become clogged and accumulate a foul-smelling mass inside. This leads to an irritation which the dog tries to relieve by pulling himself across the floor on his hindquarters or by licking and biting at the base of the tail. Eventually an abscess, which is quite painful, may develop. When this happens, the dog becomes listless, his eyes appear dull and he often refuses to eat and becomes constipated. On examination, the anus appears inflamed and you may even notice the skin bulging over the glands. Veterinarians state that a large number of dogs brought in for treatment have impacted anal glands and the owners are completely unaware of what the problem is. Usually, when a dog starts scooting across the floor on his haunches, the owner consults a veterinarian, thinking that the dog has worms.

The anal glands should be checked periodically for impaction. How often you need to do this depends on the frequency of accumulation in each dog, and each seems to be an individual where the anal glands are concerned. Some dogs need monthly attention, others may go from two to three months without any accumulation, and many dogs never need to have their anal glands emptied. Impaction is more common in Toys, probably because they are fed softer food than the larger varieties that eat bulkier foods which produce stiffer fecal matter.

When clogged glands are suspected, they must be squeezed to discharge the accumulation inside. Expressing the anals is not a pleasant job, but it must be done to prevent further infection. If you plan to bathe your Poodle, check the glands immediately before putting him into the tub, or do it just after you stand him in the water, since the accumulation is so foul-smelling.

To properly empty the anal glands, stand the dog on the grooming table or in the tub. Hold the tail up with your hand (**A**). Cover the anus with a piece of cotton because the accumulation will spurt out when the glands are squeezed. Place the thumb and index finger of your other hand in the position shown in (**B**), and gently squeeze your fingers together. If the glands have been clogged for some time, the secretion may come out like toothpaste from a tube instead of spurting. Be gentle, and don't squeeze with a heavy hand. Usually when the glands are clogged, just the slightest pressure will release the fluid. If the glands seem difficult to express, try to put your thumb and index finger under and firmly in back of the glands, then squeeze in an upward and outward motion.

If the dog is not to be bathed and there is an odor after the glands have been attended to, moisten some fresh cotton with warm, soapy water, and clean the skin and hair.

The color of the normal anal secretion is brownish-yellow. If pus or blood is noticed on the cotton, consult your veterinarian, for in case of serious infection, antibiotics will be necessary.

You should also be aware that Poodles and other long-haired breeds suffer from outward impaction. If your dog has a soft bowel movement, some of it might cling to the hair around the anus and form a mass. The mass can harden and seal the anal opening so securely, making

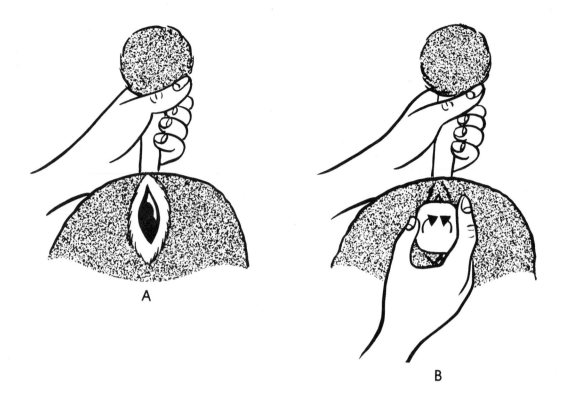

A

B

another bowel movement impossible. To remedy this situation, soak the tangled hair in warm water until the mass softens and can be removed. When the hair is dry, apply an antibiotic ointment to the area.

EXTERNAL PARASITES AND THEIR CONTROL

FLEAS, TICKS AND LICE are the most common external parasites and can infest a Poodle at any time of year. They multiply rapidly and can quickly become a serious health problem. If you are neglectful and don't take steps to destroy the parasites, your dog may be stricken with some other serious illness because his physical condition has deteriorated.

Understanding the life cycle of each external parasite is an important part of control. Killing parasites on the dog is only part of a somewhat unpleasant job. The other, and more important part, is control of larvae in your home and yard to prevent reinfestation.

If you are a professional groomer, incidentally, always isolate an infested dog until it has been attended to. Parasites spread quickly (the flea is able to jump as high as 18 inches). Don't cage an infested pet near other dogs in your salon to be groomed. After the infested dog is treated with an insecticidal product, its cage must be thoroughly disinfected before putting another dog inside. Every piece of equipment used on the infested dog must be cleaned and disinfected before being used again.

Fleas

Fleas are tiny brown blood-sucking parasites. They are quite difficult to see on Poodles because they bury themselves in the coat and dart quickly about. The first sign may be a glimpse of a small, dark bug scurrying through the coat, or the presence of small black specks on the skin or in the dog's hair. These are flea excrement, made up mostly of blood sucked from the dog, passed through the flea's digestive system and eliminated as dried blood.

Dogs pick up fleas in damp, grassy, or wooded areas, and from direct contact with infested dogs. Once they find a host, they bite the dog's skin and

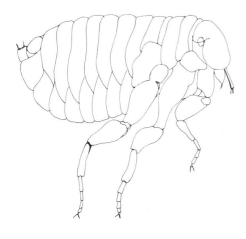

Flea

live on his blood. A flea bites by sticking its syringe-like mouth into the skin and sucking the dog's blood into its stomach. During this feeding process, the flea deposits saliva under the skin which causes the dog to itch considerably. Dogs sometimes develop hypersensitivity to the flea saliva, resulting in a condition known as Flea Allergy Dermatitis, in which the dog's persistent scratching and biting destroys the coat and causes the skin (generally on the back near the tail, the abdomen, and between the legs) to become red and thick and infested). Flea Allergy Dermatitis must be treated by a veterinarian. Fleas are dangerous, too, because they act as intermediate host of a tapeworm species that infects dogs.

The life cycle of the flea comprises four stages: egg, larva, pupa, and adult. Adult fleas lay eggs on the host dog's body, and these usually fall off to the floor or in the dog's bedding to hatch. The eggs develop into larvae within two to twelve days, depending on the temperature and humidity. The maggot-like larvae grow in dark, warm places (carpeting, floor cracks, the dog's bedding, under furniture, etc.) feeding on food crumbs and animal hairs. Next, they spin small cocoons, and within about two weeks, hatch into adult fleas.

Both the dog and his environment must be treated to effectively control fleas. Select one of the following methods:

Aerosol Flea Spray or Flea Powder. When using an aerosol insecticide, read label directions carefully before applying the product. When dusting with a powder, work it into the hair for maximum effectiveness.

Insecticidal Shampoo. These are special oil-based shampoos designed to rid the dog of fleas and ticks. The killing agent in most of these products is pyrethrins, a natural ingredient extracted from African flowers, that is safe and highly effective for use on puppies as well as adult dogs. Before using any

insecticidal product, place a drop or two of mineral oil into each eye and coat the genitals with Vaseline. Follow instructions in the Bathing Chapter, massaging the shampoo into the hair until the entire body is covered. Allow the lather to remain on the coat for at least ten minutes for maximum effectiveness, then rinse thoroughly, and dry as usual.

Flea/Tick Dip. These are concentrated liquid insecticidal products that are mixed with water *carefully,* according to package directions. The best time to dip a Poodle is immediately after a shampoo. Follow instructions for bathing, and use a regular shampoo. After the final rinse, take the dog out of the tub and towel the excess moisture from the coat. Prepare the dip according to package directions. Put the dog back into the tub. Using a plastic cup, start at the neck and pour the mixture down the back and over the sides of the body and legs. Keep pouring solution over the dog until all areas are saturated. Don't forget the hard-to-get spots under the ears, down the chest, and between the front and back legs. When working above the eyes, place your free hand over them and tilt the head upward and backward to make the dip roll down the back of the neck and nor forward, into the eyes. Use a washcloth to apply dip to the face. Do not rinse the hair after the dip is applied. Remove the dog from the tub and dry as usual.

To help prevent reinfestation, treat all the areas of your home where the dog spends a great deal of time. Vacuum his bedding, your furniture and the rugs. Clean the cracks in the floor and around the baseboards. Apply an indoor insecticidal spray to the furniture, rugs, drapes, and the dog's bed. If the house is severely infested, use an indoor fumigant fogger, designed to reach hard-to-get areas (follow directions carefully) or consult a pest control expert. Lawn and kennel dusts help to reduce the possibilities of your dog carrying parasites back into the house.

For added protection, wear a flea collar with vaporizing agents designed to kill fleas/ticks for up to 4 or 5 months. Read the manufacturer's directions carefully. While the collar is on the dog, inspect the skin regularly for redness or other signs of irritation, and consult your veterinarian if they appear.

Ticks

Ticks come in many different species, two of which primarily infest dogs: the *Brown Dog Tick,* the most common variety, which seldom bites humans and carries no human disease, and the *American Dog Tick,* which carries Rocky Mountain

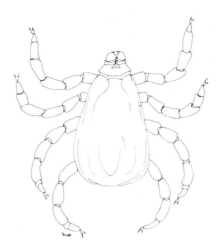

The brown dog tick.

Spotted Fever and does bite humans. Dogs pick up ticks from infested premises or by running through woods, fields, grass, damp areas and sandy beaches. The ticks attach themselves to the dog's skin and feed on his blood. Once mating has occurred, the female remains attached for several days, sucking the dog's blood and enlarging up to ten times her normal size. Then the female drops off her host and moves to a dark, quiet spot to lay eggs. Each adult female can lay from 1,000 to 5,000 eggs at one time. They hatch into larvae after an incubation period of from 3 to 8 weeks, depending on temperature and humidity. To complete their life cycle, the larvae molt into nymphs, then they, in turn, molt into adults. The new ticks look for a host to feed on, but they can live in your house up to two years without attaching themselves to a dog.

When a tick bites a dog, it forces its barbed mouth deep into the dog's skin. The barbs on the mouth prevent the tick from being easily pulled out. Tick bites are painful and extremely irritating to a dog. The irritation leads to intense itching and persistent scratching, which often results in secondary skin infections. Ticks can cause a dog to become anemic quickly because they ingest so much blood. Follow these steps to remove ticks present on the dog:

1. Examine the dog thoroughly to locate all ticks. Check any small lumps on the skin; they may be ticks. Check between the feet, inside the ears, and other hard-to-reach areas where ticks love to hide.

2. Soak all visible ticks in alcohol or a small amount of tick spray. This will help paralyze and asphyxiate the tick, causing it to loosen its barbed-mouth grip.

3. Remove any ticks in a way that will not increase the possibility of spreading Rocky Mountain Spotted Fever. All parts of the tick must be pulled out; it should not be crushed, and the person removing the tick must not touch it with bare hands.

4. Carefully grasp each tick with a tweezers or forceps. Shield your hand with paper if you use your fingers. Pull straight outward—do not twist the tick—to remove it. Do not leave the tick's head buried in the skin; it may cause infection.

5. Swab the skin with antiseptic after the ticks are removed.

6. As soon as all ticks are pulled from the dog, burn them or flush them down the toilet. Don't crush them.

7. Shampoo or dip the dog following instructions previously mentioned.

8. Disinfect the dog's bedding and spray the baseboards, carpets, floor cracks, etc., with a non-toxic insecticide. Stubborn cases of tick infestation may have to be turned over to a pest control expert who possesses both the know-how and proper insecticides to do the job.

9. For added protection, wear a flea/tick collar with vaporizing agents designed to kill external parasites for several months. Read the manufacturer's directions carefully before applying the collar.

Lice

Lice, small and pale-colored, are not as common as fleas and ticks. Dogs can be infested with sucking or biting lice, and they spread by direct contact. Lice are usually difficult to see in Poodle hair, because they are less than 1/10th of an inch long. Biting lice move down slowly through the hair, while sucking lice attach themselves to the dog's skin (usually under the ears and on the back of the neck), and feed on his blood. Lice spend their entire life cycle on the dog. Adult females produce large numbers of transparent eggs or "nits," which stick to the dog's hair. The eggs hatch and complete their life cycle in about 4 weeks, depending on the temperature and humidity. Lice are dangerous, too, because they act as a carrier of a tapeworm species that infects dogs.

To remove lice, use an insecticidal shampoo or dip, and follow instructions previously mentioned. You may have to give several shampoos or dips over a period of a few weeks to destroy new lice that are developing from eggs. For more effective results on Poodles, remove the long hair with clippers before shampooing or dipping. Even though lice spend their entire cycle on the dog's body, vacuum and disinfect his bedding and the surrounding areas to prevent reinfestation.

1

The Official AKC Standard
for the Poodle

(and some special tips for grooming in accordance with it)

THE OFFICIAL STANDARD for the Poodle is a description of the ideal of the breed, approved by The American Kennel Club. It is divided into sections defining General Appearance, Carriage and Condition; Head and Expression; Neck and Shoulders; Body; Tail; Legs; Feet; Coat; Color, and Gait. Each of these sections is assigned a certain point value (totaling 100) when the Poodle is judged in the breed ring. The Poodle Standard also describes the size of each variety and lists major faults and disqualifications. Read the standard, link the sections together, and you have a conception of the ideal Poodle.

To be an expert groomer, your first prerequisite is to know what a good Poodle looks like. You must learn to evaluate each dog individually and learn how to recognize his good points and his faults. All dogs have weak points. The perfect Poodle is yet to be born, but your objective in grooming any dog is to heighten the overall balance, good proportions and other sound points and try to conceal any imperfections he may have.

The Poodle Standard appears below in italics. After each section, there is a brief explanation to help you understand the meaning of the official words, photographs to show some Poodle rights and wrongs, and grooming tips to help disguise some major faults. These are mostly tips for pet grooming, because a prospective show exhibitor is only fooling himself or herself by showing an inferior specimen. All the camouflaging in the world is not going to fool a knowledgeable judge! But even with a structurally sound Poodle, you have to know how to stress his virtues and minimize his weak points. Inferior grooming and conditioning can slow down or spoil altogether a prospective champion's chances.

GENERAL APPEARANCE, CARRIAGE AND CONDITION — That of a very active, intelligent and elegant-appearing dog, squarely built, well proportioned, moving soundly and carrying himself proudly. Properly clipped in the traditional fashion and carefully groomed, the Poodle has about him an air of distinction and dignity peculiar to himself.

Active, intelligent, and elegant are explicit words which describe the character and appearance of the ideal Poodle. Although Poodles today are generally regarded as pets or show dogs, and officially classified in the Non-Sporting Group, they still possess the physical abilities which made them remarkable water and land retrievers centuries ago. Since ancient times, the Poodle has been bred for intelligence. The dictionary defines elegant as "graceful, refined, polished and tasteful," and this is the key to the Poodle's personality and appearance. He is elegant from top to bottom and he carries himself proudly and gracefully because he knows it (**1**)! His movement is fluid; never awkward or clumsy. He carries his head and tail high, and he is squarely-built. A well-proportioned Poodle would fit in a box: he should measure the same from breastbone to point of rump as he does from the top of the shoulder to the ground.

HEAD AND EXPRESSION — (a) Skull — Moderately rounded, with a slight but definite stop. Cheekbones and muscles flat. Length from occiput to stop about the same as length of muzzle.

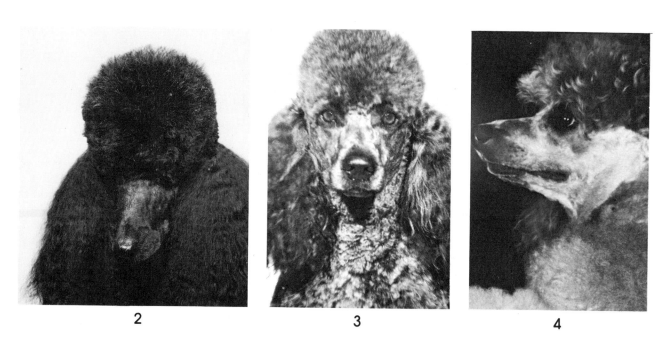

2   3   4

The ideal head is lean and slightly peaked (**2**), not wide or dome-like. The skull should not be coarse or broad at the sides of the forehead. The "stop" refers to the step-up from the nose to the skull. The stop should begin at the corners of the eyes, not below or above them. The Poodle should have smooth, flat cheeks. Major faults are thick skull, or one which is coarse at the sides of the forehead (**3**); high bridge between the eyes; wedge-shaped head; and cheekiness, a term meaning prominent cheekbones which bulge past the eyes (**4**).

Grooming Tips: On all the pet styles, the Poodle's head may be shaped round or slightly squared. But the topknot should be scissored full, and never wedge-shaped, broad or flat. Study the topknot section before you scissor the head. Poor grooming on a Poodle's topknot will detract from a good head.

(b) MUZZLE — Long, straight and fine, with slight chiseling under the eyes. Strong without lippiness. The chin definite enough to preclude snipiness. Teeth white, strong, and with a scissors bite.

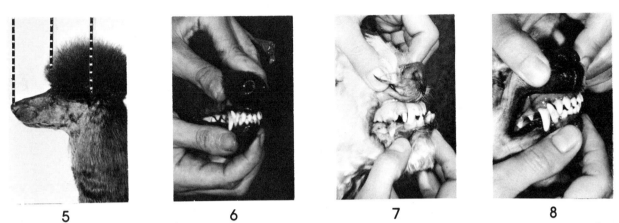

5   6   7   8

Ideally, the distance from the ear to the corner of the eye should be almost the same as the length from the eye to the end of the muzzle (**5**). The slight molding under the eye should look as though it has almost been chiselled. "Snipiness" means lack of sufficient underjaw. When you look at a snipey dog in profile, you see only the top of the muzzle. "Lippiness" means a heavy upper lip, common on the Spaniels, which hangs over the lower lip. (**6**) shows a scissors bite. (**7**) shows an undershot bite, where the front teeth of the lower jaw project beyond the front teeth of the upper jaw when the Poodle's mouth is closed. (**8**) shows an overshot bite, where the incisors of the upper jaw overlap and do not touch the front teeth of the lower jaw when the mouth is closed.

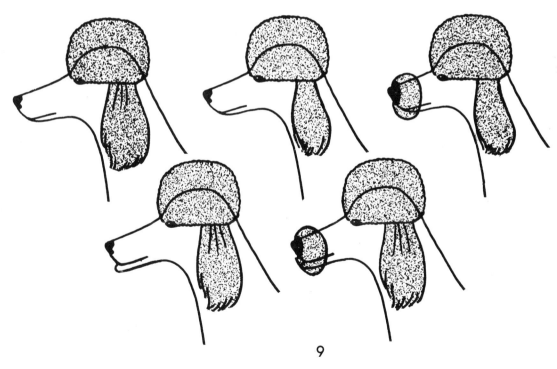

9

Grooming Tips: A pet Poodle with a short muzzle looks better without a moustache. Clipping the face clean adds as much length as possible, while a moustache shortens the face. A Poodle with large round eyes, or one with a snipey muzzle or protruding teeth looks better with a moustache. Always keep the moustache close to the nose and away from the corners of the mouth, to make it look neat. The sketches in (**9**) illustrate these statements.

(c) EYES — Very dark, oval in shape and set far enough apart and positioned to create an alert intelligent expression.

The eyes should be oval-shaped and very dark, ranging from a deep brown in black Poodles to a slightly lighter brown (but not orange or yellow) in the dilute colors. More information on eye color is found in the *Color* section of the Standard. Faults include round, bulging eyes (**10**); eyes set too far apart which gives the dog an unintelligent expression; and eyes too light in color or showing too much white.

(d) EARS — Hanging close to the head, set at or slightly below eye level. The ear leather is long, wide, and thickly feathered; however, the ear fringe should not be of excessive length.

A Poodle's ears should be set on a line level with the corners of the eyes or slightly lower, but never higher. The hair on the ear is called the feathering, while the ear itself is called the leather. The leathers are almost fan-shaped. They hang close to the head and, on the best Poodles, almost reach the nose when pulled forward.

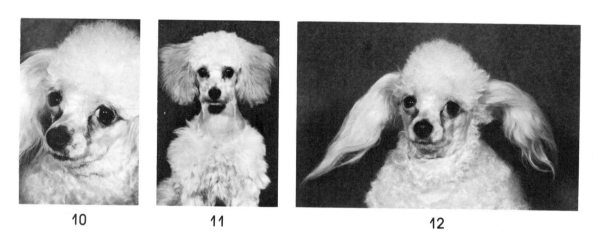

10   11   12

Major faults are short or high-set ears (**11**); ears placed too far back on the head; and flying ears. Flying ears are a common fault on Toy and small Miniature Poodles; the leathers are short, set horizontally, and stand out from the head as shown in (**12**).

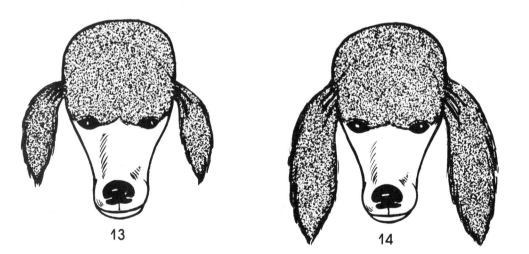

13   14

Grooming Tips: Never clip short or high-set ears. Always let the feathering grow as long as possible. Instead of scissoring a definite separation between the ears and topknot, blend the feathering into the topknot hair, as shown in (**13**) and (**14**) to help disguise these faults.

NECK AND SHOULDERS — Neck well proportioned, strong and long enough to permit the head to be carried high and with dignity. Skin snug at the throat. The neck rises from strong, smoothly muscled shoulders. The shoulder blade is well laid back and approximately the same length as the upper foreleg.

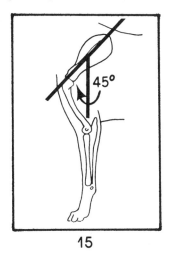

15

16

The neck should be well-arched, strong and in balance with the head and body. A short, thick neck makes a Poodle appear coarse. A very long neck gives the impression of weakness and affects the dog's overall balance. To explain a well-proportioned neck, first locate the withers on the Anatomy Chart which is on Page 13. The withers are the seven vertebrae that join the neck to the back. The distance from the skull to the withers should measure from about one-quarter to one-third as long as the dog measures in height at the withers.

Shoulder blades should slope back at almost a 45-degree angle (**15**). The rounded upper ends of the blades should be close to the withers. The shoulder blades should never be set higher than the withers, since the withers are a part of the backbone and the highest part of the body. Without sound, well-laid-back shoulders, the Poodle's front assembly will be imperfect and his movement poor.

Major faults are ewe neck (concave curvature at the top neckline); short and flabby neck (**16**); and shoulders which do not slope back at a 45-degree angle.

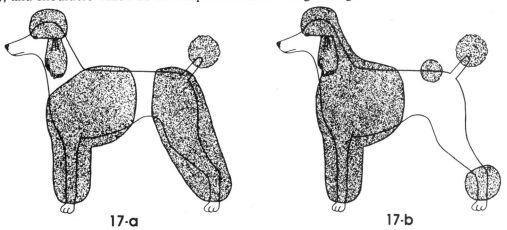

17-a   17-b

Grooming Tips: It's hard to disguise a short neck, but to add length to one that is not fat, choose a pet pattern where the hair is clipped off both sides of the neck (**17-a**). The Dutch, Royal Dutch, New Yorker, and Sweetheart are good choices for Poodles with short (but not stocky) necks. If the neck is short and fat, choose the Sporting, Kennel, or any pattern with hair on the back of the neck, as shown in (**17-b**). Clip or scissor the hair short on the back of the neck, clip the throat a bit lower in the front, then shape the topknot slightly higher, to add length.

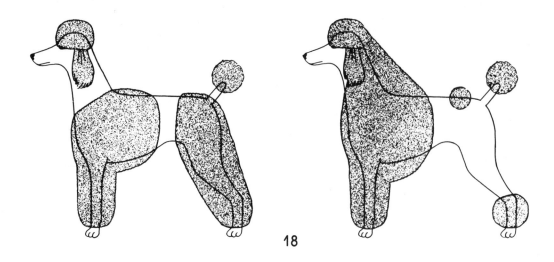

18

To make a long neck look shorter, choose a pet pattern where the hair remains on the back of the neck, instead of clipping the neck completely, as shown in (18). The Kennel, Lamb, Miami, Mandarin, and the pet variations of the show clips are fine for Poodles with overly long necks. If you do use a style where the throat and back of the neck are clipped, choose the Mink Collar, or shape the topknot into a "V" at the back of the neck on any of the other pet clips.

BODY — To insure the desirable squarely-built appearance, the length of body measured from the breastbone to the point of the rump approximates the height from the highest point of the shoulders to the ground. (a) Chest — Deep and moderately wide with well sprung ribs. (b) Back — The topline is level, neither sloping nor roached, from the highest point of the shoulder blade to the base of the tail, with the exception of a slight hollow just behind the shoulder. The loin is short, broad and muscular.

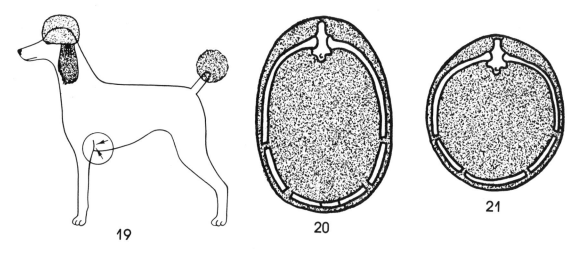

19   20   21

Depth of chest is best judged from a side view of the Poodle (19). The brisket line should be almost even with the elbows and run parallel to the ground back to the eighth rib. Use your hands to feel the rib spring. The correct shape of the rib-cage is similar to that of an overturned rowboat (20), not barrel-like (21).

The back should be short and as level as possible. If you run your hand from the shoulder to the base of the tail, other than a slight hollow just behind the shoulder, you should feel no humps. The loins should be strong and muscular. Hipbones must not protrude and should be level with the spine. If you place your hand on the lower back and push down, the Poodle should be able to support himself against this pressure without sagging. The croup should be level. When the hindquarters slope too sharply, it gives the Poodle a low tail set and swings the rear framework under the body.

22   23   24

Major faults are long back (**22**); roach back (**23**), usually accompanied by a low tail set; sway back, which often causes the tail to curl over the back; shallow chest (**24**), and flat ribs.

Grooming Tips: Pet Poodles with long bodies look best in styles that make the body appear shorter. The Bandero, Chicago Dutch, Pittsburgh Dutch, Pajama Dutch, Hollywood and Sweetheart are good choices for long-bodied dogs. In the sketches above, notice how the Dutch pattern, with a clipped line going from the base of the skull down the center of the back almost to the end of the tail, adds length to the body. Then look at the Bandero Clip and see how this pattern makes a long body appear slightly shorter.

Pet Poodles with short bodies and very long legs look best in patterns that make the body appear longer. The Dutch, Royal Dutch, Criss-Cross Dutch and New Yorker are good styles for short bodied dogs. The sketches show how the Royal Dutch pattern adds length to the body, while the Hollywood pattern tends to shorten the body.

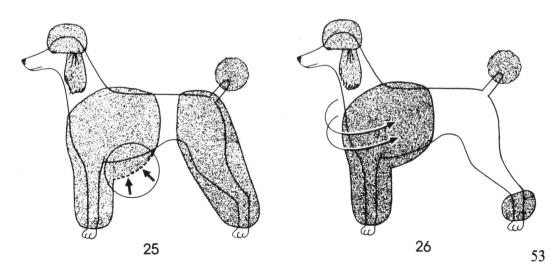

25   26

Never scissor the Poodle's body to look flat-sided. Follow the natural contour of the body, rounding the hair over the ribs and hindquarters. If your Poodle has a shallow or flat chest, gradually increase the length of hair over the ribs and under the chest when scissoring (**25**).

Shape the chest rounded, from shoulder to shoulder, as shown in (**26**).

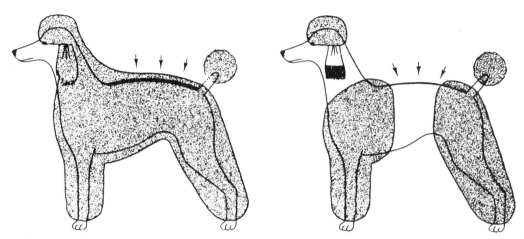

Puppies often have protruding hipbones and a curved back before maturing. If your puppy looks this way, postpone clipping him in a fancy pattern until he is more mature. If you have an older dog with a roach back, choose the Puppy, Kennel, Sporting or Lamp clip instead of a fancy pattern, as shown in the sketches above. Scissor the hair to make the back look straight.

TAIL — Straight, set on high and carried up, docked of sufficient length to insure a balanced outline.

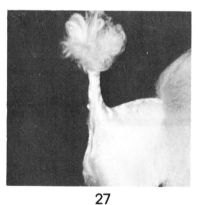

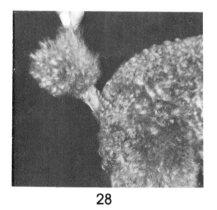

27   28

The tail should be set at the end of the backbone (**27**). Major faults include low-set tails (**28**); tails that are not carried gaily, but down between the legs; and tails that curl up and are carried over the back (squirrel tails).

Grooming Tips: Sketches and instructions for camouflaging improperly docked tails are found under *Instructions for Clipping the Poodle's Tail* on Page 64.

LEGS — (a) Forelegs — Straight and parallel when viewed from the front. When viewed from the side the elbow is directly below the highest point of the shoulder. The pasterns are strong. Bone and muscle of both forelegs and hindlegs are in proportion to size of dog.

Forelegs should appear straight when viewed from the front of the Poodle (**29**), but stand under the body when viewed from the side (**30**). The elbows should be directly below the highest point of the shoulder blades, close to the sides of the body and should not turn in or

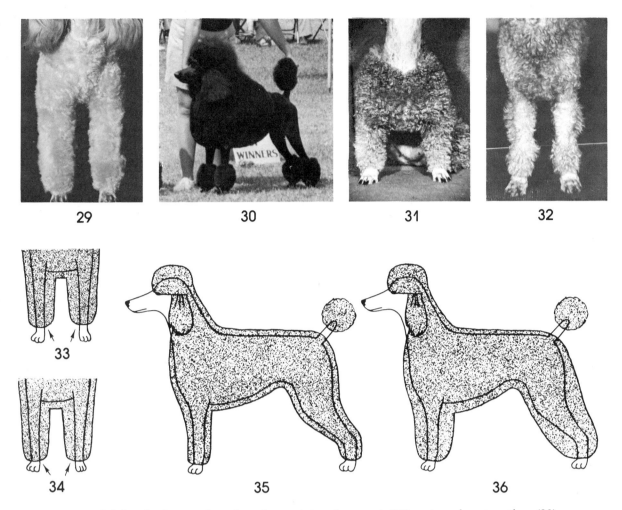

29   30   31   32

33

34   35   36

out. Major faults are short legs; legs set too far apart (31) or too close together (32).

Grooming Tips: To make short legs look longer, never expose any part of the ankle with clippers (33). Always clip to the end of the foot 34). Scissor the leg hair short. Then shorten the hair over the ribs and under the chest, instead of leaving the coat long, as shown in (35) and (36). Try not to trim bracelets or puffs on short legs.

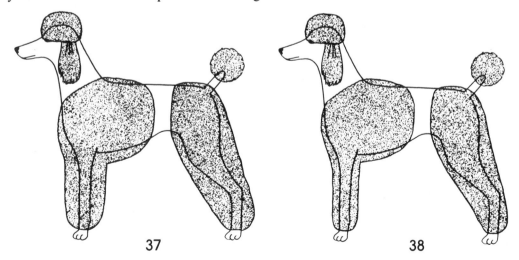

37   38

To make long legs look shorter, gradually increase the length of hair over the ribs and under the chest (37), instead of leaving the hair short (38). The hair on the legs should be left full and scissored into a full shape, following the Poodle's natural conformation by emphasizing angulation above the hock joint and the curve of the stifle joint. Do not taper the hair at the ankles.

55

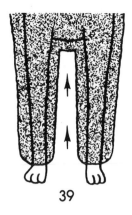

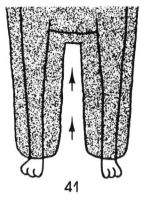

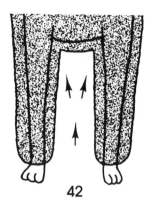

39

40

41

42

If the legs are too close together, leave more hair on the outside of each leg and shorten the hair on the inside **(39)**, instead of scissoring as usual **(40)**. If the legs are too far apart, leave more hair on the insides and shorten the hair on the outsides **(41)**, instead of scissoring as usual **(42)**.

(b) HINDLEGS — Straight and parallel when viewed from the rear. Muscular with width in the region of the stifles which are well bent; femur and tibia are about equal in length; hock to heel short and perpendicular to the ground. When standing, the rear toes are only slightly behind the point of rump. The angulation of the hindquarters balances that of the forequarters.

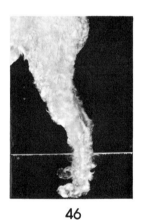

43

44

45

46

When you look at the side view of the back legs, they should be well-angulated with a definite bend at the stifle joint and again at the hock joint **(43)**. The thighs should be well-developed. The hocks must not be bent or curved and should not turn in or out. They should be perpendicular and close to the ground. When viewing the dog from the side, the bones from the stifle joint to the hock joint are longer than the bones from the hock joint to the ground.

Faults are short legs; cow hocks, which turn in and cause the feet to turn out **(44)**; sickle hocks, which are bent or curved and not straight **(45)**; legs set too close together or too far apart; thin upper thighs with poor bone and muscle **(46)**.

56

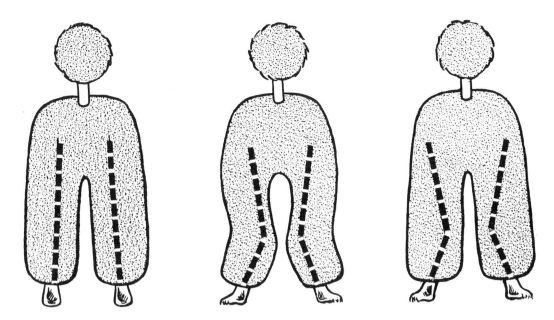

Grooming Tips: From a rear view, the hindlegs should look straight up and down. When scissoring a cowhocked dog, leave more hair on the outside of the leg where the hock turns in, and less hair on the inside, to make the leg look straight, as shown in the sketches below. Shorten or lengthen the hair to camouflage short or long legs.

FEET — The feet are rather small, oval in shape with toes well arched and cushioned on thick firm pads. Nails short but not excessively shortened. The feet turn neither in nor out. Dewclaws may be removed.

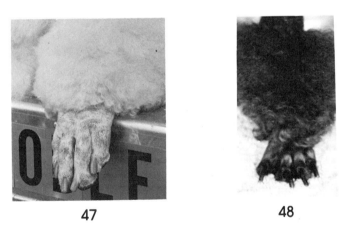

47   48

A Poodle should have neat, oval, elegant looking feet. The ideal foot is rather small, tight and highly arched (**47**). Major faults include flat feet with spread toes (**48**) and thin pads.

COAT—
(a) Quality — (1) curly: of naturally harsh texture, dense throughout. (2) corded: hanging in tight even cords of varying length; longer on mane or body coat, head, and ears; shorter on puffs, bracelets, and pompons.

The correct texture of a curly coat is harsh and profuse, not silky. The mane coat should be thick and profuse and never separated. The pack should be dense and plush. Bracelets should look dense and not ragged or droopy. Poodle coat texture is usually at a peak when the dog is between two to five years old. Faults include woolly or silky-textured coats.
Grooming Tips: Texture and condition of coat should determine what pattern you select for a pet Poodle. A dog with a thick, harsh coat can be trimmed in any pattern, plain or fancy,

and will look good. A dog with a poor coat should always be trimmed in an easy-to-do, uncomplicated pattern, and the hair should be scissored short.

(b) Clip — A Poodle under 12 months may be shown in the "puppy" clip. In all regular classes, Poodles 12 months or over must be shown in the "English Saddle" or "Continental" clip. In the Stud Dog and Brood Bitch classes and in a non-competitive Parade of Champions, Poodles may be shown in the "Sporting" clip. A Poodle shown in any other type of clip shall be disqualified.

(1) "Puppy": A Poodle under a year old that may be shown in the "Puppy" clip with the coat long. The face, throat, and base of the tail are shaved. The entire shaven foot is visible. There is a pompon on the end of the tail. In order to give a neat appearance and a smooth unbroken line, shaping of the coat is permissible.

(2) "English Saddle": In the "English Saddle" clip, the face, throat, feet, forelegs and base of the tail are shaved, leaving puffs on the forelegs and a pompon on the end of the tail. The hindquarters are covered with a short blanket of hair except for a curved shaved area on each flank and two shaved bands on each hindleg. The entire shaven foot and a portion of the shaven leg above the puff are visible. The rest of the body is left in full coat but may be shaped in order to insure overall balance.

(3) "Continental": In the "Continental" clip the face, throat, feet and base of the tail are shaved. The hindquarters are shaved with pompons (optional) on the hips. The legs are shaved, leaving bracelets on the hindlegs and puffs on the forelegs. There is a pompon on the end of the tail. The entire shaven foot and a portion of the shaven foreleg above the puff are visible. The rest of the body is left in full coat but may be shaped in order to insure overall balance.

(4) "Sporting": In the "Sporting" clip a Poodle shall be shown with face, feet, throat, and base of tail shaved, leaving a scissored cap on the top of the head and a pompon on the end of the tail. The rest of the body and legs are clipped or scissored to follow the outline of the dog, leaving a short blanket of coat no longer than one inch in length. The hair on the legs may be slightly longer than that on the body.

In all clips, the hair of the topknot may be left free or held in place by no more than three elastic bands. The hair is only of sufficient length to present a smooth outline.

As stated above, these are the only patterns recognized in the American breed ring. If your Poodle is a pet or to be shown in the Obedience ring, he may be clipped in any style.

COLOR — The coat is an even and solid color at the skin. In blues, grays, silvers, browns, cafe-au-laits, apricots, and creams the coat may show varying shades of the same color. This is frequently present in the somewhat darker feathering of the ears and in the tipping of the ruff. While clear colors are definitely preferred, such natural variation in the shading of the coat is not to be considered a fault. Brown and cafe-au-lait Poodles have liver-colored noses, eye rims and lips, dark toenails and dark amber eyes. Black, blue, gray, silver, cream and white Poodles have black noses, eye rims and lips, black or self-colored toenails and very dark eyes. In the apricots while the foregoing coloring is preferred, liver-colored noses, eye rims and lips, and amber eyes are permitted but are not desirable.

Parti-colored dogs shall be disqualified. The coat of a parti-colored dog is not an even solid color at the skin but is of two or more colors.

Blotchy skin on light-colored dogs and unsound colors are not desirable. Parti-colored Poodles are disqualified in the show ring. No coats may be colored or touched up in any way for the show ring.

GAIT — *A straightforward trot with light springy action and strong hindquarters drive. Head and tail carried up. Sound effortless movement is essential.*

Good Poodle movement is smooth and effortless with the head and tail carried high. A Poodle must be soundly constructed to move properly; no dog with major faults will move with light, springy action.

Faults are wobbly movement; tight movement; toeing in or out; paddling, a term meaning movement with the front feet wide and swinging outward and causing a rolling front action; and "hackney gait," a high stepping action caused by straight shoulders lacking the proper layback.

SIZE —

The Standard Poodle is over 15 inches at the highest point of the shoulders. Any Poodle which is 15 inches or less in height shall be disqualified from competition as a Standard Poodle.

The Miniature Poodle is 15 inches or under at the highest point of the shoulders, with a minimum height in excess of 10 inches. Any Poodle which is over 15 inches or is 10 inches or less at the highest point of the shoulders shall be disqualified from competition as a Miniature Poodle.

The Toy Poodle is 10 inches or under at the highest point of the shoulders.

Any Poodle which is more than 10 inches at the highest point of the shoulders shall be disqualified from competition as a Toy Poodle.

VALUE OF POINTS —

General appearance, temperament, carriage and condition *30*
Head, expression, ears, eye, and teeth *20*
Body, neck, legs, feet and tail *20*
Gait *20*
Coat, color and texture *10*

MAJOR FAULTS — *Any distinct deviation from the desired characteristics described in the Breed Standard with particular attention to the following:*

Temperament — *Shyness or sharpness.*

Muzzle — *Undershot, overshot, wry mouth, lack of chin.*

Eyes — *Round, protruding, large, or very light.*

Pigment — *Color of nose, lips and eye rims incomplete, or of wrong color for color of dog.*

Neck and Shoulders — *Ewe neck, steep shoulders.*

Tail — *Set low, curled, or carried over the back.*

Hindquarters — *Cow hocks.*

Feet — *Paper or splayfoot.*

DISQUALIFICATIONS

Clip — *A dog in any type of clip other than those listed under Coat shall be disqualified.*

Parti-colors—*The coat of a parti-colored dog is not an even solid color at the skin but of two or more colors. Parti-colored dogs shall be disqualified.*

Size — *A dog over or under the height limits specified shall be disqualified.*

— Approved November 14, 1978

How to Use the Clipping Instructions

IF YOU HAVE STUDIED each preceding section of this book, you should have a thorough knowledge of the preliminaries of Poodle grooming: the necessary equipment, handling tips, brushing, combing, coat care, bathing, fluff drying, dealing with external parasites and, most important of all, the description of the ideal Poodle. Now you are ready to begin clipping.

Before turning to the following pages, read these suggestions to help you better understand the grooming instructions:

1. Basic instructions for clipping the feet, face, tail and stomach; moustache styles; ear styles, and topknot styles precede the body pattern instructions. These parts are clipped the same way, whichever pattern you select.

2. If you plan to show your Poodle in the breed ring, concentrate on the Show Clips section. In all regular classes, Poodles under 12 months may be shown in the "Puppy" clip. Poodles over 12 months must be shown in either the "Continental" or "English Saddle" clip. A Poodle in any other trim will be disqualified. The Standard adds, however, that in the Stud Dog and Brood Bitch classes and in the non-competitive Parade of Champions, Poodles may be shown in the "Sporting" clip.

3. If you plan to show your Poodle in the Obedience ring, he may be clipped in any style.

4. Don't be surprised to see so many Poodle patterns for pets. Many are variations of clips you may already know. These variations differ from the original pattern in some minor way, usually a different leg style. It would be impossible to list every variation for each of the basic clips. All variations, however, regardless of the clip they follow, may be used on any other pet clip in this book.

5. The Show Clips appear first, followed by the Pet Clips. The easy-to-do pet clips, such as the Kennel, Sporting, Lamb, Miami, Summer Miami, precede the patterns which require more intricate body clipping, such as the Dutch, New Yorker, Sweetheart, Bandero, Diamond, Mink Collar and their variations.

6. This book stresses a very important point—*setting pattern lines at specific bones.* You can use the same pattern instructions to clip any variety—Toy, Miniature, or Standard—and not worry about correct proportions. To explain further, let's use the instructions for the Dutch Clip as an example. When clipping down the back of the neck, the instructions state to clip from the base of the skull down to the shoulders, but never below them. If you were clipping a Toy Poodle, the distance from the base of the skull to the shoulders may be two inches. On a Miniature, the distance may be three inches. On a Standard Poodle, the distance may be 4 to 5 inches. By following instructions to clip from the bone to bone, no specific measurement is necessary, yet the pattern is in perfect proportion to the Poodle variety you are clipping. When you clip the front part of the pattern, known as the "jacket," the instructions tell you to clip the jacket line around the last rib. Thus, the jacket is formed between the shoulders and the last rib. If you're clipping a Toy Poodle, the distance from the shoulders to the last rib may be 4 inches. On a Miniature, the distance may be 5 to 6 inches. On a Standard, the distance may be 9 to 10 inches. Again, by following instructions to clip around the last rib, the jacket is in perfect proportion of any size of Poodle. If you follow directions, you will not set a pattern that is out of proportion.

60

7. When width of the clipper blade is important to the Poodle's size, specific mention is made in the clipping instructions.

8. On all pet clips, there is no definite rule for the length of the hair. The coat on the body, legs, and topknot can be as long or as short as you wish, depending on your preference. Toy Poodles look best with about one and one-half to two inches of hair, and Standard Poodles, from two to three inches of hair. Leave more hair if you prefer a full coat or less hair if you like a short clip.

CLIPPER BURN

Clipper burn is a painful sore or rash which sometimes inflames the sensitive areas (face, throat, underside of the tail, and genitals) of Poodles after clipping. Many Poodles suffer from clipper burn every time they are clipped, while others are never bothered. Generally, white and light-colored Poodles seem to be more affected than those of darker colors.

Clipper burn progresses like a chain reaction. First, the skin becomes red and irritated, then the dog starts scratching. If the irritated areas are ignored and not treated at this stage, the dog continues to scratch until the tender areas become raw with painful, open sores. To prevent clipper burn on a sensitive Poodle:

1. Don't use a fine blade on the sensitive areas of a young dog. Remember, you can always take more hair off, but you can't put it back. Always use a #10 blade when clipping a sensitive Poodle.

2. Do not clip any sensitive areas before shampooing. Instead, bathe the dog with a medicated shampoo which will help to control clipper burn.

3. When clipping sensitive parts after the dog is shampooed and dried, be sure the clipper blade is clean and cool. *Never clip a sensitive Poodle with a hot blade.* As you clip, test the blade by placing it against your wrist. If it feels hot to the touch, spray the blade with an aerosol "cooling" product.

4. When clipping the sensitive areas, always hold the clipper blade *flat* against the skin. Never point the edges of the blade into the dog's skin. This is a common reason for clipper burn on the genital area of male Poodles. Clipping underneath the back legs is an awkward job and, if the groomer holds his or her clippers at a slight angle instead of flat against the skin, it could cause enough irritation to start the dog scratching.

5. Do not use a dull blade or one with missing teeth to clip the sensitive areas.

6. When the dog's nails are trimmed, smooth the rough edges of each nail immediately with a file or emery board. One reason why clipper burn is a problem on the face is because a Poodle can scratch that part easily. Think of the irritation that rough nail edges can cause!

7. As soon as the sensitive areas are clipped, dab them with an "after-clip" lotion for dogs or Bactine (available in any pharmacy) to prevent irritation. The product you use should be greaseless, so the dog will not try to rub it off.

8. Advanced cases of clipper burn (open sores or scabs) will require treatment by a veterinarian. Don't delay!

CLIPPING THE FEET

CLIPPING THE FEET is the most difficult part of Poodle grooming for beginners. Because this is a ticklish spot, your dog may fuss the first few times you try to clip him. Don't become frustrated. Treat him gently, clip his feet often, and he will soon become accustomed to it.

With the exception of the underside of the back feet, all clipping work is best done with the dog in a sitting position, with the foot you are trimming pulled slightly forward. The dog is comfortable in this position because his weight rests on his other three legs. If your Poodle breaks the "sit" position at any time, immediately put him back into place. Firmly command him to sit, then proceed with the clipping. Be patient! Don't be rough to the dog to try to make him behave during the clipping process. He will be frightened and will not cooperate the next time he is groomed.

Clip the Poodle's feet with a #15, #30 or any of the narrow cutting blades. Do not use a #10 blade; it will not clip close enough to clean the hair between the toes.

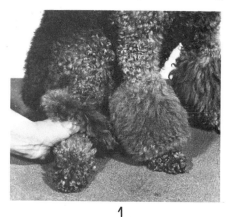

1

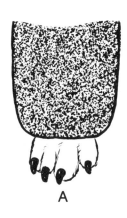

A

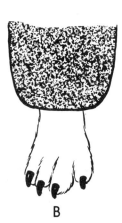

B

Begin by placing your dog on a sturdy grooming table. Work on the back feet first. Pull the left back foot forward, close to the front leg (**Photo 1**). Pointing clippers upward, start near the nails and clip off all the hair on the top of the foot (**Photo 2**). Clip only to the end of the foot (**Sketch A**). The mistake most beginners make is clipping too high up on the ankle (**Sketch B**).

Now comes the difficult part for beginners, clipping the hair between the toes. The secret of doing this without cutting the skin is to spread the webbing between the toes. On the underside of your Poodle's foot, there is one large pad and four small toe pads. To spread the webbing correctly, put your second finger in between the large pad and four small pads. At the same time (**Photo 3**), use your thumb to spread the toes apart on the top of the foot. Now clip the hair between the toes with the edge of the clipper blade in the position shown in **Photo 4**. You will not cut the foot if you spread the webbing and clip with the edge of the blade. Clip the top of the other back foot.

The underside of each back foot is clipped with the Poodle in a standing position with the leg pulled back, as shown in **Photo 5**. Clip only to the end of the foot, making sure that the clipped line evenly encircles the leg. Spread the toes apart with your thumb and second finger, as shown in **Photo 6**, and clip the hair between the pads.

Clip the front feet with the Poodle in a sitting position, facing you. As you did on the back feet, take the paw in your hand and pull it forward, as shown in **Photo 7**. Start near the nails and clip the hair off the top of the paw. Clip only to the end of the foot.

62

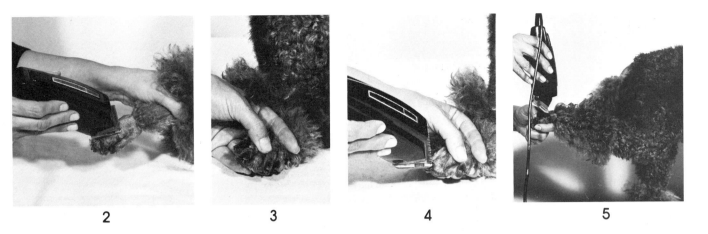

2   3   4   5

Clean the hair between the toes exactly as you did on the back feet. Put your second finger between the toe pads underneath and your thumb on top of the foot to spread the webbing. Remove all hair between the toes with the edge of the clipper blade.

The underside of the front foot is clipped with the dog in a sitting position. Pull the foot forward. Clip to the end of the foot, making your clipped line evenly encircle the ankle. Then spread the toes apart with your thumb and second finger, as shown in **Photo 8**, and clip the hair from between the pads underneath. Clip the other front foot. Check all four feet to see that no straggly hairs remain around the nails.

You may want an assistant to steady the dog the first few times you clip the feet. He or she should support the dog from behind and extend forward the leg you are working on. The assistant should place a hand on the hock joint as you clip the back foot, and at the elbow while you clip the front foot.

Photo 9 shows the Poodle in a grooming sling, an aid for clipping the feet of a fussy dog. If you work alone and do not own a grooming sling, use a choke chain attached to a leather lead to control a fussy dog. Slip the chain above the elbow as you clip each front foot, or above the hock joint as you clip each back foot. Let the lead dangle to the floor. Put your foot on the lead. In this position, you can control the dog by sliding the lead forward with your foot if the dog fusses, which tightens the chain around the leg. When the dog relaxes, take your foot off the lead and the chain loosens.

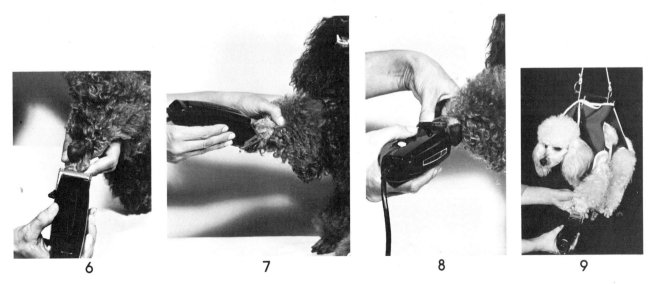

6   7   8   9

CLIPPING THE POODLE'S TAIL

CLIPPING THE POODLE'S TAIL is very easy. Use a #10 blade on pet Poodles or a #15 if the dog can take a closer clip. Use a #15 or #30 if the dog will be in show clip. The area to be clipped depends on the length of the tail, but generally speaking, it measures about one to one and one-half inches of a Toy Poodle, about two inches on a Miniature Poodle, and about three inches on a Standard, depending on the conformation of your dog. If the tail is properly docked, most groomers divide it in half, clipping one part and using the other part for the pompon.

1

2

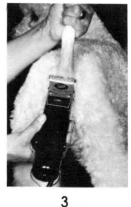
3

4

Begin by holding the end of the tail with your free hand. Starting in the middle of the tail stump, clip the top side of the tail toward the body, as shown in **Photo 1**. Clip only to the juncture of the tail and the body. Start again at the middle of the tail, as shown in **Photo 2**, and clip the sides the same way. The underside of the tail is a delicate area and is clipped in the opposite direction, from the body out to the pompon, as shown in **Photo 3**. The clipped line around the middle of the tail must be even or the shape of the pompon will not be round.

Gently clip around the anal opening, as shown in **Photo 4**. Do not use clippers below the anus unless you are planning to use the Continental, Summer Miami or other clip in which the hair is shaved from the hindquarters. The hair below the anus is shortened with scissors, not clipped, on all styles which have hair on the back legs.

Before shaping the pompon, either **(a)** comb the hair toward the tail tip, or **(b)** grasp the hair at the tip and twist it. Then scissor straight across the ends of the hair to remove any excess.

On the pet clips, the pompon at the end of the tail is scissored into a round shape. The secret of achieving the correct shape is to fluff out the hair with a comb before you scissor. If you scissor without first combing the hair, you will end up with a wedge-shaped pompon.

Hold up the end of the tail with your free hand, then fluff out the hair with a comb, almost as if you were "back combing" it, as shown in **Photo 5**. Begin scissoring (with straight or curved shears) on the underside of the pompon, as shown in **Figure 6**. Hold the scissors flat as you take

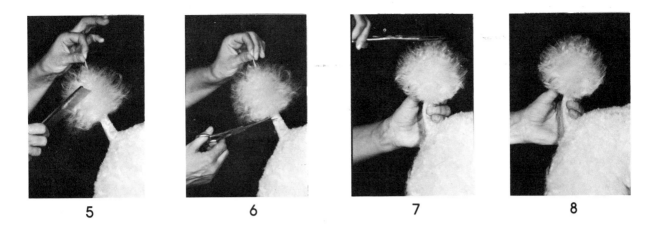

5	6	7	8

off a little hair at a time. Scissor completely around the pompon, as shown in **Photo 7,** shaping it into a round ball. **Photo 8** shows the finished results. On the show clips, the tails basically are round but much fuller, usually at the top, to add the proper balance to the clip. Ideally, after scissoring, the tail pompon should be as high as the Poodle's head.

Many Poodles have improperly docked tails and an expert groomer must know how to deal with this problem:

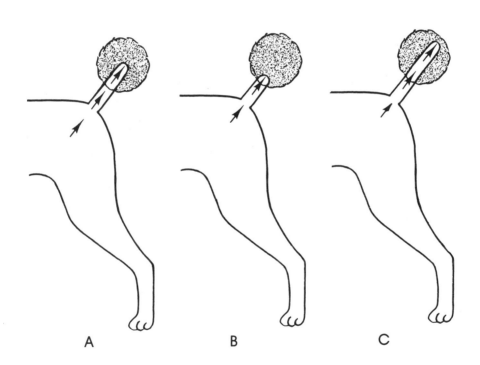

A	B	C

Sketch A shows a normal tail with the correct amount of clipped area. The tail is divided in half. The bottom half is clipped to the point where the tail joins the body, and the top half is used for the pompon.

Sketch B shows how to disguise a short tail (a common problem). Move the pompon out toward the tail tip, allowing more clipped area to create the illusion of a longer tail.

Sketch C shows how a long tail can be shortened by reducing the amount of clipped areas.

CLIPPING THE POODLE'S FACE

THE POODLE'S FACE may be clipped clean or left with a moustache. Poodles shown in the breed ring in the Puppy, English Saddle or Continental Clips must have clean shaven faces. On all other styles, a moustache is optional. You simply select the style you like best.

The face is always clipped with the dog in a sitting position, facing you. Each time your dog fusses and tries to move from this position during the clipping, immediately put him back into place. Firmly command him to sit, then start clipping again. He will soon understand what is expected of him.

The face is always clipped by using the clippers against the growth of hair, from the head to the nose. Be sure you use the correct blade to clip the face. It is a sensitive area that is easily burned if clipped too closely. To get the best results, use a #15 blade. If your dog is a puppy, or an older dog with sensitive skin, use a #10 blade. Use a #30, only if your dog can take a close clip. Do not use a close cutting blade on a dog you have never clipped. Remember, you are clipping against the growth of hair and the clip will be close, even with a #15 blade.

Instructions and photographs for clipping the face clean are given in Section A. Instructions and sketches for the popular moustache styles are given in Section B.

A. Clipping The Face Clean

1   2   3

Sit the Poodle on the grooming table, facing you. If you are right handed, begin clipping the side of the face at your right. If you are left handed, do the opposite. Turn the ear back and, with the edge of the clipper blade, clip a straight line from the ear to the corner of the eye, as shown in **Photo 1**. This line automatically becomes the topknot line on each side of the face. Always clip to the corner of the eye, not above it or below it. Clip off all hair in front of the ear, as shown in **Photo 2**, to make the ear lie as close to the head as possible. Stretch the skin at the corner of the eye upward and backward with your free thumb, as shown in **Photo 3**, and clip under the eye. Do not take off any hair above the Poodle's eyes with the clippers.

4   5   6   7

Continue clipping forward on the cheek and side of the face. To avoid cutting the folds of skin at the corner of the mouth, use your free thumb to stretch the skin back, as shown in **Photo 4**. Press the jaws firmly together and clip the remaining hair on the lips and around the nose, as shown in **Photo 5**. Turn the Poodle's head to the side, as shown in **Photo 6,** and clip the other side of the face the same way.

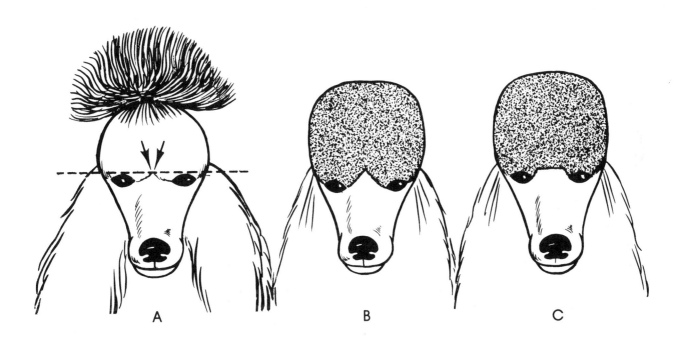

A   B   C

When both sides of the face are clipped, hold the muzzle firmly with your free hand and clip an indentation between the eyes. Clipping this indentation is often confusing for beginners. Begin at the inside corner of each eye and make an inverted V shaped cut (∧) between the eyes, using the clippers toward the muzzle, as shown in **Photo 7**. The mistake most beginners make is cutting this ∧ too deep. As shown in **Sketch (A)**, the point of the ∧ should be even with the top of the eye. However, if the head is short or stubby, make the point of the ∧ higher than the top of the eyes, as shown in **Sketch (B)**, to lengthen the head. If the head is flat on top, instead of making the inverted V-shaped cut, clip the indentation straight across, as shown in **Sketch (C),** to give the impression of more stop.

| 8 | 9 | 10 | 11 |

Clip the remaining hair on top of the nose, as shown in **Photo 8**. Clip the hair from the underside of the muzzle by lifting the head up, as shown in **Photo 9**, and clipping from the throat up to the lips.

If your Poodle tries to bite when you clip his face, use a muzzle for protection. The best grooming muzzle is a silk stocking or a strip of gauze about 12 to 15 inches long. Either material is soft and can be tied fairly tight around the dog's mouth without cutting into the skin. Wrap the center of the muzzle around the mouth and tie a knot underneath, as shown in **Photo 10**. Pull each end back under each ear and tie the muzzle again at the base of the skull, as shown in **Photo 11**. Now you can easily clip the face by sliding the muzzle forward or backward.

B. Clipping the Face with a Moustache

Sit the Poodle on the grooming table, facing you. Following instructions in Section A, clip each side of the face to within 1 to 2 inches of the nose (or about half-way between the corner of the mouth and the nose). Clip the inverted V between the eyes. Clip the hair on top of the nose down as far as the clipped line on the sides of the face. Clip the hair on the underside of the muzzle up as far as the clipped line on each side of the face.

REMEMBER: The moustache must never be set close to the corner of the mouth, because it would be too large and bushy and spoil the Poodle's expression. Keep the moustache close to the nose to show traces of the tapered muzzle. The three most popular moustache styles are the French, German and Donut. Select the style you prefer and follow instructions:

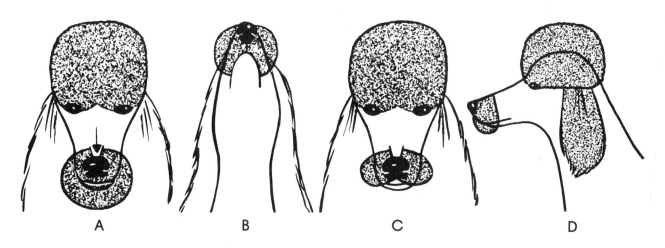

| A | B | C | D |

The French Moustache

On this style, the whiskers stick out from the sides of the nose. The hair on the lower jaw and top of the nose is clipped off. Begin by removing the hair from the top of the nose, as shown in **Sketch A.** Hold the dog's head up and clip the hair from the underside of the muzzle, as shown in **Sketch B.** Comb the hair on each side of the nose straight out, and scissor to an even length of from one half inch to one inch. **Sketches C** and **D** show the finished front and side view of the French Moustache.

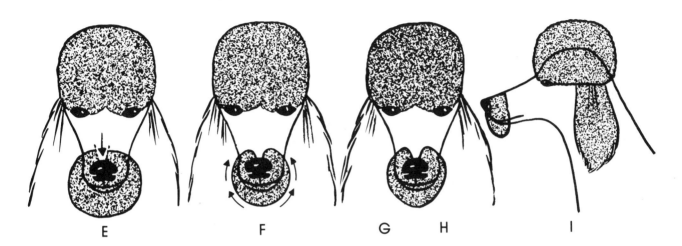

The German Moustache

This style has hair on each side of the nose and under the jaw. Only the top of the nose is clipped clean. As shown in **Sketch E,** begin by clipping the top of the nose. Comb the hair and scissor the moustache round, as shown in **Sketch F,** or tapered, as shown in **Sketch G. Sketches H** and **I** show the finished front and side view of the German Moustache.

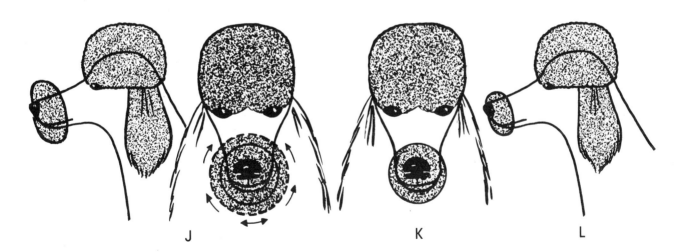

The Donut Moustache

This style has the same length of hair on the top and sides of the nose and under the jaw. If you have clipped the face to within one to two inches of the nose as instructed, you need only comb the hair and scissor a round shape as shown in **Sketch J.** Remember to leave the same amount of hair on all sides of the nose and under the jaw, to make this moustache look like a "donut." **Sketches K** and **L** show the front and side view of the Donut Moustache.

CLIPPING THE STOMACH

  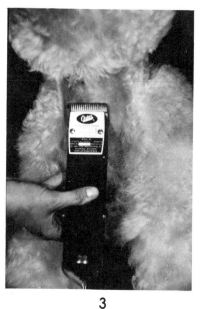

1   2   3

THE CORRECT POSITION for clipping the stomach depends on the size of your Poodle. Use a #15 blade to clip the stomach. If your dog has sensitive skin, use a #10. It is easier to clip underneath a small Poodle by holding up the front legs with your free hand, as shown in **Photo 1**. A large dog should stand on the grooming table with the hindquarters facing you. Clip the right side of the stomach by lifting the right rear leg, as shown in **Photo 2,** then clip the left side of the stomach by lifting the left rear leg.

For all pet patterns, you should clip the stomach up to the last rib. Pointing clippers upward, start just above the testicles or vulva and clip to the middle of the dog, stopping at the last rib, as shown in **Photo 3.** Clip gently around the nipples or penis without applying pressure to the clipper.

Before clipping the stomach for the show patterns, be sure to study the pattern instructions and determine where you will set the line for the long hair of the ruff. The ruff is set in back of the last rib, at a spot that will make the dog look balanced. Once this line has been established, clip the stomach up to this point. The ruff will then completely encircle the body.

TOPKNOT STYLES

IF YOU INTEND TO SHOW your Poodle in the breed ring, the topknot is not shaped. Instead, the long forelocks are fastened back with a latex band. For tying back the forelocks see the Puppy, English Saddle and Continental Clip instructions.

   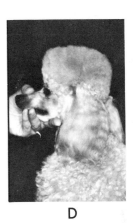

A	B	C	D

On the pet clips, there are two basic head styles for the Poodle—round and sqaure. **A** and **B** show the front and side views of the Round Topknot. **C** and **D** show the front and side views of the Square Topknot. The topknot shape is a matter of personal preference. Select the shape you like best for any of the patterns.

The Poodle must sit on the grooming table, facing you, for all topknot work. The groomer must see both sides of the head while using the scissors to get an evenly-shaped topknot. Brush the head thoroughly before beginning any work on the head. Then, because the brush flattens the hair, comb the topknot upward and forward, using light strokes to lift the hair, rather than flatten it. You are now ready to begin scissoring a round or square topknot.

Round Shape

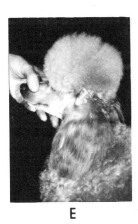 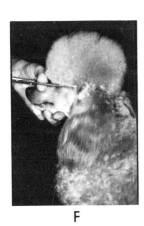 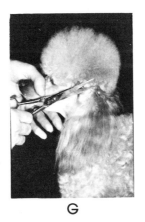 

E	F	G	H

Hold the dog's muzzle with your free hand (**E**). Begin scissoring the topknot hair at the corner of the eye and work back to the ear. Begin at the right side if you are right handed. Begin at the left side if you are left handed. Cut off all the hair that falls over the clipped line from the eye to the ear (**F**). Continue scissoring back over the ear (**G**) and around the base of the skull (**H**) to

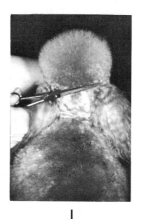

| I | J | K | L |

the opposite ear (**I**), taking a little hair off at a time. Do not pull out the hair with your fingers. If you are not satisfied with your shaping, recomb the hair upward and forward and begin scissoring again.

Return to the corner of the eye where you first started scissoring (**J**). This time, however, scissor around the front of the head to the opposite ear, shaping the topknot round, as shown in (**K**). Scissor the front of the topknot even with the eyes. (**L**) is the front of the topknot in profile view, showing the topknot hair even with the eye line. The hair never extends past the eyes.

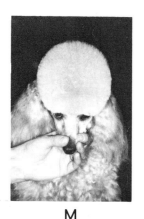

| M | N | O | P |

When you have completely scissored around the head, shape the rest of the topknot into the "dome" shape shown in (**M**), leaving more hair in the center of the head and tapering the sides. The hair at the deepest point of the round topknot is about one and one-half inches long on Toy Poodles, two to two and one-half inches long on Miniature Poodles, and three to three and one-half inches long on Standard Poodles. If the dog's coat is soft and silky, scissor the hair shorter than the above measurements.

(**N**) shows the finished round topknot. (**O**) shows the back of the topknot, rounded at the base of the skull. (**P**) shows another way to clip the back of the topknot by centering a point on the back of the neck. This point extends about one-half inch below the base of the skull on Toy Poodles, three quarters inch to one inch below the base of the skull on Miniature Poodles, and two inches below the base of the skull on Standard Poodles.

Square Shape

Hold the dog's muzzle with your free hand (**Q**). Start scissoring the topknot hair at the corner of the eye and work back to the ear. Cut off all hair that falls over the clipped line from the eye to the ear (**R**). Continue scissoring back over the ear (**S**) and around the base of the skull (**T**)

72

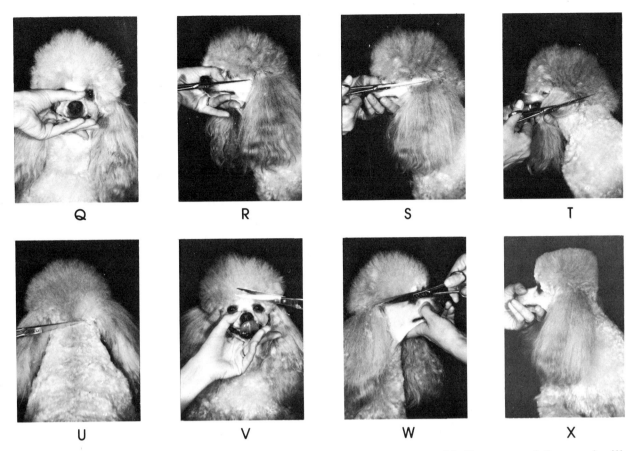

Q   R   S   T

U   V   W   X

to the opposite ear (**U**). Even though you want a square topknot, this line around the nead will be round, following the natural contour of the skull. The square shape is emphasized at the top of this head style.

Return to the corner of the eye where you first started scissoring (**V**). This time, scissor around the front of the head to the opposite ear (**W**). Scissor the front of the topknot even with the eyes. (**X**) shows the front of the topknot in profile view. No hair extends past the eye line.

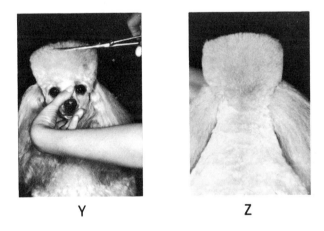

Y   Z

(**Y**) shows how to shape the head square on top. Do not round or taper the top of the head or you will lose the square shape. The hair at the deepest point of the topknot should be about one and one-half inches long on Toys, two to two and one-half inches long on Miniatures and three to three and one-half inches long on Standards. If the coat is soft and silky, scissor the hair shorter than the above measurements.

(**Z**) shows the finished square topknot. This style can also be used with the point centered in the back of the neck.

73

EAR STYLES

THE POODLE'S EARS may be clipped in many different styles. They may be clipped short to resemble Terrier ears, left with full feathering, or tasseled. On each of the pet clips, the ear style is a matter of personal preference. You simply select the style you like best. If you intend showing your Poodle in the breed ring, the ears are never clipped. Only the bottom edges may be scissored to create a more balanced outline.

Terrier Ears

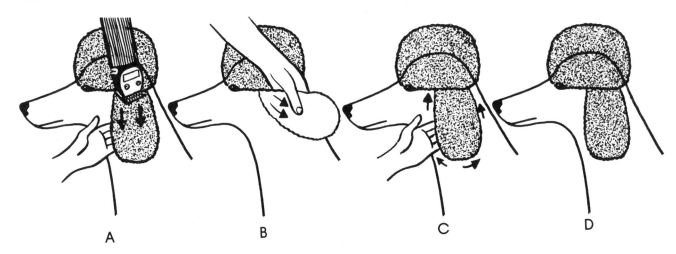

A   B   C   D

Terrier ears are especially attractive with the Kennel, Sporting, Miami and Summer Miami Clips. The hair is shortened to an even length of one-half inch. This is an excellent style for country Poodles. Sit the Poodle on the grooming table, facing you. Use a #5 blade. Lay the ear flat on the palm of your hand. Start clippers at the top of the ear and clip down to the end of the leather. Clip the outside of the ear (**A**). Then clip the inside of the ear (**B**). Hold the ear with your free hand and scissor the sides (**C**). Clip the opposite ear. The finished Terrier ear style is shown in (**D**).

Full Feathering

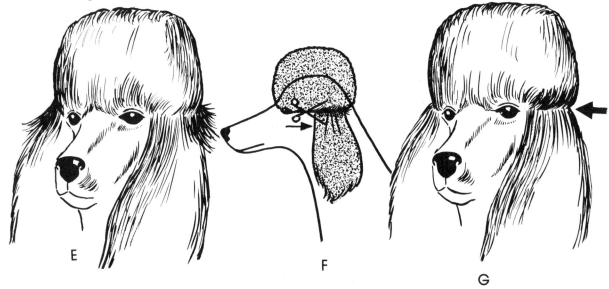

E   F   G

74

If the ears are left with full feathering and not clipped, scissor a slight indentation at the top of the ear, to show a definite separation between the ear and the topknot. Too much straggly hair at the top of each ear will make the Poodle's head look enormous. Scissoring a separation refines the outline of the head. Sit the Poodle on the grooming table, facing you. After the topknot is scissored, brush the ear feathering. (E) shows a front view of the ears before scissoring the indentation. Hold the dog's muzzle in your free hand. With scissors, begin at the top of each ear, and shorten the hair (F). (G) shows a front view of the ears with the scissored indentation.

Clipping Tassels on the Ears

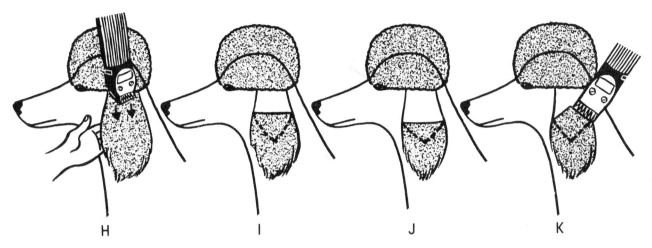

H   I   J   K

Sit the Poodle on the grooming table, facing you. Use a #15 blade. Always use the clippers in one direction, from the top of the ear downward. Never turn them the opposite way or you will cut the flaps of skin on each side of the leather and injure the ear. If you are right handed, begin clipping the ear at your right side. If you are left handed, begin at the left side. Lay the ear flat on the palm of your hand. Start at the top of the ear and clip down (H). If you like a full tassel, clip to the middle of the ear (I). If you prefer a bare ear, clip to within one inch of the end of the leather (J). (K) shows how to slant the clippers if you wish to make the tassel bell shaped. Clip the inside of the ear as far down as you clipped the outside (L). Hold the ear with your free hand and scissor along the edges to remove the shaggy hairs (M). Clip the opposite ear. Brush the tassels. The tassels may be left long (N), or scissored to a length of from one to two inches (O).

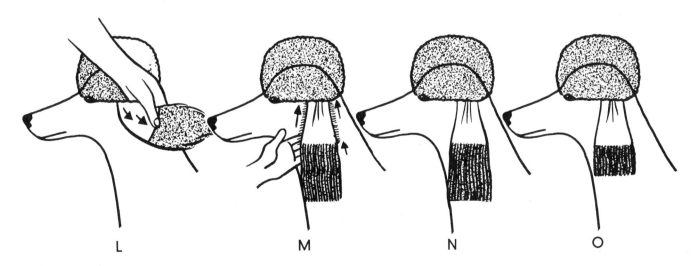

L   M   N   O

Introduction
to the
Show Clipping Section

ONE OF THE MOST DIFFICULT PARTS of writing a Poodle trimming book is explaining show grooming. It's perplexing, because of several variables. When you show a Poodle in the breed ring, you are competing with seasoned exhibitors and handlers. Unless you want to become quickly disillusioned, you must learn to match their talents in handling as well as grooming. Each dog is an individual and no one is faultless. Therefore, even assuming that you own a fine specimen, you must evaluate your dog truthfully, and then learn what is necessary to stress his virtues and minimize his weak points. Now fantastic handling and grooming will not make a poor specimen into a top winning dog. But inferior grooming and conditioning, and casual presentation can slow down or even defeat a prospective champion's chances. Problem number one is that while it is possible to show what the Puppy, the Continental and English Saddle clips look like, and to generally explain how they are achieved, the way you actually clip and scissor them on Poodles will vary slightly depending on each dog's conformation.

Another problem is learning what is fashionable in Poodle grooming at the pre-sent time. Fashion, in dog talk, means the kind of dog being exhibited (subtle changes occur in every breed through the years). And this term may also be used for the style in which a dog is presented. You need only to glance at the following photographs to see how show grooming has changed over the past few decades. In the 1930's and 1940's, Poodles were not very plush looking. In the 1950's and 1960's, there were shown with outrageously long mane coats (reaching down to the puffs on the forelegs), dripping with topknot and ear feathering. In the 1970's, exhibitors and handlers began presenting Poodles with shorter, rounder mane coats, topknots and ear feathering, enhancing the overall balance and elegance of the breed.

Attend as many puppy matches and dog shows as possible in your area. Plan to arrive well in advance of Poodle judging time. Go to the grooming area and observe the handlers and exhibitors closely. You will learn a great deal by watching how they prepare their Poodles before they take them in the ring. Go to ringside and carefully watch the Poodles being shown. The more you observe, the more you will learn!

The Changing Fashions of Show Trims

Show trim of the '30s.

The '40s.

The early '50s.

The late '50s.

The '60s.

Into the '80s.

The Puppy Clip

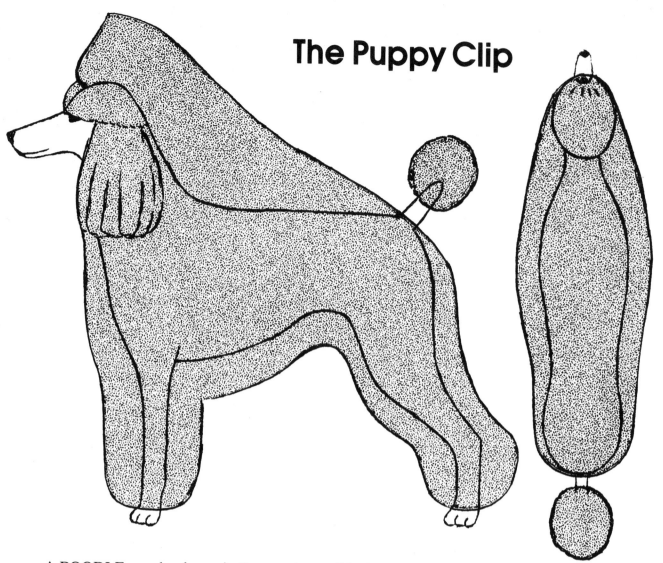

A POODLE may be shown in Puppy trim until he is 12 months of age. Then he must be shown in either the English Saddle or Continental clip. Correct brushing and coat care is a most important part of show grooming. Be sure to study thoroughly the advice in *Coat Care for the Show Poodle.*

A

1. Follow instructions for clipping the feet. Clip only to the end of the feet and don't make the mistake of exposing any part of the ankles.
2. Follow instructions for clipping the face. On the sides of the head, be sure the clipped line is straight between the outside corner of the eye to the ear.
3. Follow instructions for trimming the tail.
4. Follow instructions for clipping the stomach.
5. Place the Poodle in a sitting position facing you to clip the throat (**Sketch A**). It should be trimmed into a "V" shape. Start at a point at the middle of the throat, about one inch below the Adam's Apple on a Toy Poodle, about one and one-half inches on a Miniature, and about two inches on a Standard, and clip each side of the neck up to the front of the ear. Adjust these measurements slightly depending on your Poodle's length of neck, if necessary.

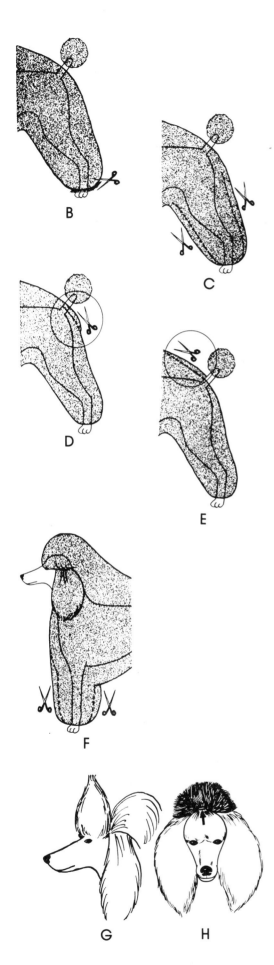

B

C

D

E

F

G   H

6. The Poodle standard states that *"in order to give a neat appearance and a smooth, unbroken line, shaping of the coat is permissible"* on the Puppy trim. While the scissoring work on the Puppy trim is easy to do, it can be difficult to explain. Study the accompanying illustration. Actually, very little hair is scissored off the body with the exception of the hindquarters and around the base of the tail. The rest of the coat remains long, with only the untidy top hair scissored off to get the shape you see in the illustration. As a puppy's coat grows long to be trimmed into the English Saddle or Continental at one year, the ends become straggly. The tips of these untidy ends should be scissored off every four to six weeks to keep the coat in shape and strengthen the hair. This type of scissor work is called "tipping" and does not greatly alter the length of coat. Consider it a sort of pruning. If you let a bush grow wild, its strength dissipates, but when you prune it, the branches grow stronger and healthier. That, in effect, is what you are doing to the Puppy's hair.

    Begin scissoring the rear end first. Stand the puppy on the grooming table with hindquarters facing you. Start by shaping the back legs. If you are right handed, do the leg at your right. If you are left handed, start at the left side. Comb the hair downward and outward, as the puppy coat naturally falls. Scissor off any hairs that fall below the clipped line around the foot **(B)**. Then tip and shape the leg. Start at the ankle and work up to the point where the back leg joins the body, no higher for the moment. When you finish tipping one part of the leg, begin again at the ankle and trim another section up to this point. Work completely around the leg in this manner **(C)**, following the Poodle's natural conformation, emphasizing angulation above the hock joint and at the curve of the stifle. Lift the opposite leg to scissor any hard-to-reach areas on the inside of the leg. If you are not satisfied with your tipping, recomb the hair and begin again. Scissor tip the other back leg, making it even in size and shape.

7. Next, shape the hair on the hindquarters and around the base of the tail. Every Poodle exhibitor has his or her favorite way of trimming this part and, if you are a beginner, the easiest way is to comb the body hair up and out to fluff the coat. Begin scissoring upward from where the back leg joins the body. Shape the hair below the base of the tail short but round, to keep the puppy from looking long-bodied **(D)**. As you scissor from the tail toward the hipbones **(E)**, gradually increase the length of hair.

A show prospect before and after his first puppy clip.

With each method, the hindquarters should be shaped to blend gradually into the longer hair. There should be no signs of a break in the mane coat.

8. The remaining hair on the body is tipped slightly with scissors to remove untidy ends.

9. Comb the hair on the front legs downward and outward, as it naturally falls. Scissor off the straggly ends that fall below the clipped line around the feet, then tip each front leg into the cylindrical shape shown in (**F**).

10. Comb the ear feathering downward.

11. Use a comb or knitting needle to part the hair across the top of the head, from in front of one ear to the front of the other. Hold the forelocks in your free hand and brush them smooth with a pin brush. Place a small latex band around the hair, close to the head. Twist the band with your fingers into a figure-eight shape and wrap it around the topknot once again. Always use a band that is small enough to turn only twice. Pull the back of the latex band backwards, away from the eyes, with your thumb and index finger, until a puff of hair forms between the eyes. Then comb the topknot upward and outward to blend with the neck hair. If short hairs above the eyes slip out of the band, a touch of hair styling gel should hold them in place. For older puppies with a great deal of coat, it may be necessary to divide the topknot into two sections. Photographs and instructions for doing this are found under the English Saddle Clip.

Most exhibitors like to spray a fine mist of coat dressing or hair spray on the topknot to keep it in place. If you wish to do this before entering the ring, never overspray with gummy lacquers which stiffen and alter the natural texture of the coat.

THE PUPPY CLIP FOR PET POODLES

For pet puppies, not being shown in the breed ring, you may scissor the hair to an even length all over the body. The topknot may be scissored round in front to keep the hair from falling into the eyes. This is an excellent choice for a Poodle's "first" clip.

The puppy clip for a pet Poodle.

The English Saddle Clip

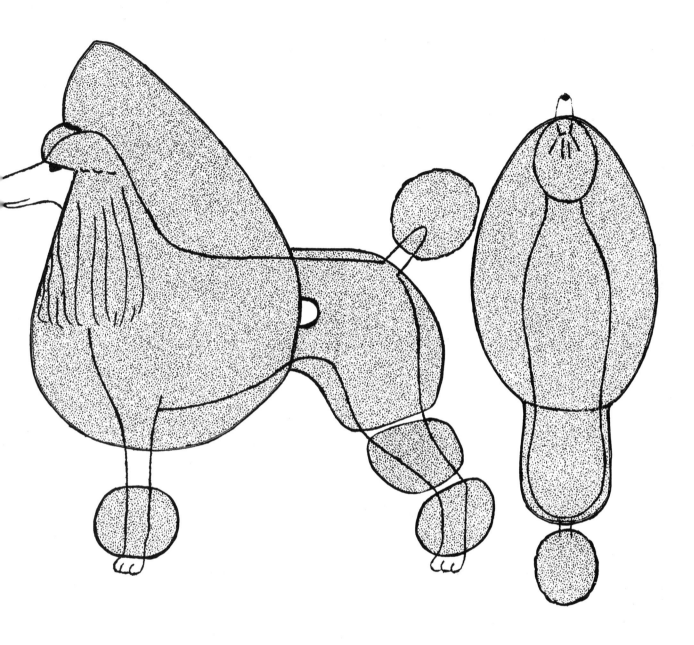

The Poodle standard states that *"in the 'English Saddle' clip, the face, throat, feet, forelegs and base of tail are shaved, leaving puffs on the forelegs and a pompon on the end of the tail. The hindquarters are covered with a short blanket of hair except for a curved shaved area on each flank and two shaved bands on each hindleg. The entire shaven foot and a portion of the shaven leg above the puff are visible. The rest of the body is left in full coat but may be shaped in order to insure overall balance."*

Correct brushing and coat care are a most important part of show grooming. Be sure to study thoroughly the advice offered in *Coat Care for the Show Poodle.*

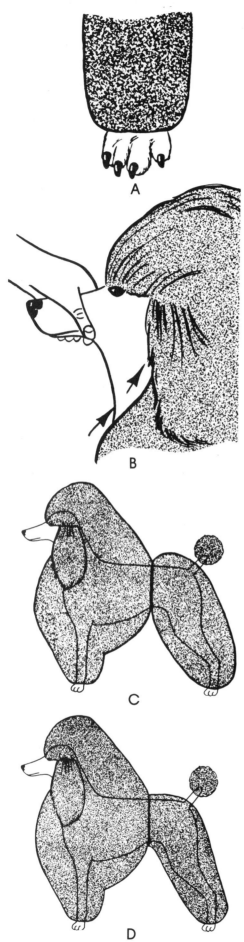

A

B

C

D

1. Follow instructions for clipping the feet. Clip only to the end of each foot (**A**) and don't make the mistake of exposing any part of the ankle.

2. Follow instructions for clipping the face. On the sides of the head, be sure the clipped line is straight between the outside corner of the eye and the ear.

3. Follow instructions for clipping and scissoring the tail.

4. Sit the Poodle on the grooming table, facing you, to clip the throat. It should be trimmed into a "V" shape. Start at a point at the middle of the throat, about one inch below the adam's apple on a Toy Poodle, about one and one-half inches on a Miniature, and about two inches on a Standard, and clip each side of the neck with a #15 blade up to the front of each ear (**B**). You may want to adjust these measurements slightly according to your dog's length of neck.

5. Stand the Poodle on the grooming table. The first step in the English Saddle trim is to make a part completely around the dog in back of the last rib (**C**), with the end-tooth of a comb or a knitting needle. The hair in front of the part, called the "mane coat" or "ruff," will remain long (to be scissored round, later on). The hair in back of the part, called the "pack," will be scissored to a length of from one-half to two inches, depending on the variety of Poodle you are trimming. It's tricky to explain exactly where on the dog's body to part the hair. It should be separated where it keeps the dog in balance, and this spot varies with the individual dog. Try making the part one-half inch in back of the last rib on a Toy Poodle, about one inch in back of the last rib on a Standard. Then step back and look at the dog. If he appears out of balance, move the part forward or backward. It's often necessary to experiment a little until the dog looks right. Once the part is made, comb the long hair in front of the part forward. To protect it and keep it out of the way while you trim the hindquarters, if you are a beginner, wrap a strip of gauze or a ribbon around the back and tie it under the chest.

6. Comb the hair on the hindquarters and back legs and scissor the hair shorter to make it easier to set the pack and bracelets. The Poodle should resemble **Sketch D**.

7. Use a #15 blade to clip the stomach. Pointing clippers upward, start just above the testicles or vulva and clip up to the part around the middle of the dog.

8. Study the illustration of the Poodle in English Saddle Clip. Notice that the hindquarters are covered with short, plush hair, except for a half-circle or crescent-

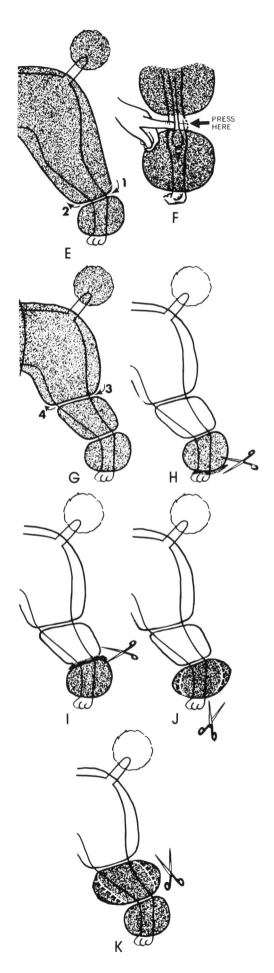

shaped clipped area on each flank and two clipped bands on each back leg. There is a bracelet below the hock joint and one above the hock joint, ending at the stifle joint. Begin by clipping the lower band to set the bottom bracelet. Starting just above the hock joint, scissor a narrow band completely around the leg from Point 1 to Point 2 (**E**). Notice in this side-view sketch that the band slopes downward from the back to the front of the leg. Then, if you are working on a Miniature or Standard Poodle (it is not necessary to clip a Toy), use one of the narrow cutting blades, or a #15 or #30, and clip carefully over the scissored area. Pointing clippers upward, trim around the leg in short strokes, making the band about one-quarter inch wide. The leg is hollowed above the hock bone, so you must place your finger on the opposite side of the leg when you clip and press the hollowed part forward, shown in **Sketch F.**

9. Clip the upper band. Use your fingers to feel for the center of the stifle joint. Scissor another band at this spot, completely around the leg, from Point 3 to Point 4 (**G**). (You may have to place the band slightly higher or lower if your Poodle is short- or long-legged.) Once again, if you are trimming a Miniature or Standard Poodle, point clippers upward (using the same blade), and clip around the leg in short strokes, making the upper band about one-quarter inch wide.

10. Clip the bands on the other hind leg. Be sure both legs are even.

11. Shape the bottom bracelet. Comb the hair down, then scissor off any untidy ends that fall below the clipped line around the foot (**H**). Then comb the hair up and scissor off the untidy hairs above the clipped band at the hock joint (**I**). Comb the hair outward, then shape the bracelet with scissors (**J**). When viewed from the side, the bottom bracelet is more oval than round, sloping downwards from the back of the leg towards the front, emphasizing angulation and well let-down hocks. It should be about one and one-half to two inches in diameter on a Toy, from two to three inches in diameter on a Miniature, and from three to four inches in diameter on a Standard. Scissor the bottom bracelet on the opposite leg even in size and shape.

12. Scissor the upper bracelet. Comb the hair down and scissor off any untidy hairs that fall below the clipped line around the hock joint. Comb the hair up and scissor off any hair that extends over the clipped band around the stifle joint. Fluff out the hair with your comb, then scissor (**K**) the bracelet into a modified oval

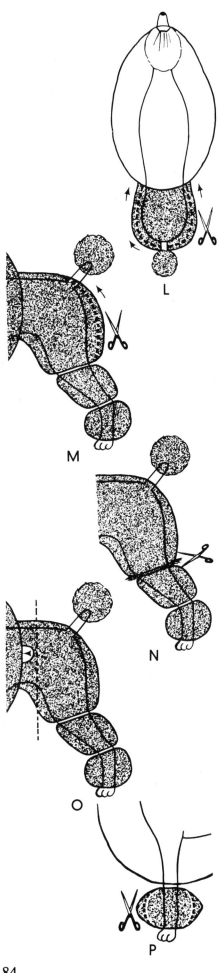

L

M

N

O

P

shape. Hold scissors flat against the hair you work on, taking a little hair off at a time. Do not dig into the coat with the scissor points. Don't pull out the hair with your fingers or you will spoil the "plush" look. If you are not satisfied with the shape of the bracelet, recomb the hair and begin scissoring again. Scissor the upper bracelet on the opposite leg even in size and shape.

13. Comb the hair on top of the pack upward. The top of the pack (**L**) and sides are shaped square and flat. It should join the mane coat with only the part line as a separation. Comb the hair outward and downward on the hindquarters under the tail. This part of the pack is scissored to appear slightly rounded (**M**), and blends gradually with the flat, squared top part in front of the tail. Comb the hair down at the clipped band around the stifle joint, then scissor off untidy hairs that fall below the shaved area (**N**).

14. To complete the pack, clip a half-circle or crescent-shaped indentation (sometimes called the "kidney patch") halfway between the top and underside of the body. Clipping the indentations can be confusing for beginners. Study the opposite sketch. The deepest part of the crescent should not extend back beyond the point where the hind leg joins the body. If you are unsure of yourself, make the shape of the indentation with chalk, or scissor the line into the hair. Then using one of the narrow cutting blades or a #30, clip the half-circle on each flank (**O**). Comb the hair near the clipped areas forward and scissor off uneven ends that obscure the crescent shape.

15. Turn the Poodle around to stand facing you to clip the puffs on the forelegs. Begin about one and one-half to two inches above the clipped line around the foot on a Toy Poodle, two to three inches above the clipped foot line on a Miniature, and about four inches on a Standard. Clip the front and sides of each foreleg up to the elbow. To take off the hair evenly, clip the back of each foreleg in the opposite direction, from the elbow down to the bracelet line. If you are a beginner and unsure about clipping, trim the bracelet line with scissors before clipping.

16. Comb the hair on each front puff. Comb the hair down and scissor around the foot to remove any straggly hairs that fall below the clipped line. Then comb the hair up, and scissor off any untidy hairs above the clipped line around the leg. Fluff out the hair with a comb, then shape the puffs. They are more rounded in shape than the bracelets on the back legs (**P**), tapering slightly at the bottom.

The topknot is fanned upward and outward. It blends with the rest of the mane coat and acts as a frame around the Poodles's face.

Q

R

17. With the Poodle in a standing position on the grooming table, comb the mane coat outward for its final scissoring. Study the illustration of the Poodle in English Saddle Clip and notice that the long ruff is shaped into a round ball. You can make shaping easier by the way you prepare the long hair. Begin by combing it upward and outward around the neck. As your hand moves backwards, comb the hair upward and slightly forward toward the head. Comb the sides of the body outward and forward. Comb the hair on the chest downward and outward, and on the underside of the dog, downward and forward. As you scissor and shape the mane coat, think of circles and balls. Most groomers find it easier to start underneath and scissor upward, shaping the ruff round. The end result should be an overall balanced Poodle. The length of the mane coat varies with the individual dog. But do be sure to trim off enough hair under the chest to show a portion of the clipped area on the forelegs between the ruff and the puffs. An excessive amount of hair under the chest or on the sides of the mane coat gives the Poodle an ungraceful look, especially when he moves about the show ring.

18. Put up the topknot with latex bands. It is always preferable to use latex rather than rubber bands in the Poodle's coat. Rubber bands exert too much pressure on the hair shaft and can eventually cause breakage. Latex bands are lighter in weight, more flexible, and offer better control. Use either of two methods to put up the topknot:

A. Part the hair with a comb or knitting needle across the top of the Poodle's head from in front of one ear to the front of the other ear (Q). Brush the hair in front of the part smooth. Place a latex band (small enough to turn only twice) around this section of hair, close to the skull. Loop the band around the topknot once again (R). Once

1

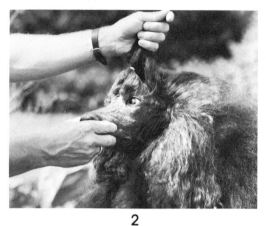

2

3

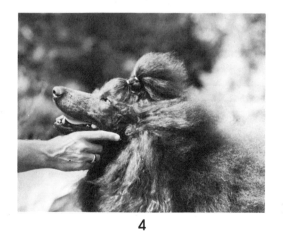

4

S

fastened, grasp the band between your thumb and index finger, then pull backwards (away from the eyes) until a puff of hair forms above the eyes. Use your comb to fan out the topknot to blend with the remaining coat on the head (**S**). If any short hairs slip out from the band above the eyes, a light touch of hair styling gel will keep them in place.

B. Brush the topknot hair smooth (**Photo 1**). Part the hair across the top of the head with a comb or knitting needle, about halfway between the ear and corner of the eye. Place a latex band (small enough to turn only twice) around this section of hair, close to the skull. Loop the band over the hair once again. Puff the hair above the eyes (**Photo 2**). Make another part across the top of the head, behind the first, from in front of one ear to the front of the other ear (**Photo 3**). Brush the hair smooth, then fasten with a latex band as you did the first section. Fasten the two sections together by looping the second hand over the first, or by using a third band (**Photo 4**). Use a comb to fan the hair upward and outward on top of the head to blend with the rest of the coat.

If the topknot is too long, it may be scissored shorter to create a better balance to the mane coat. To keep the hair in place, some exhibitors spray a fine mist of coat dressing or hair spray on the topknot. If you wish to do this before entering the ring, never overspray with gummy lacquers that stiffen and alter the natural texture of the coat.

19. Brush the ear feathering downward. Tip uneven ends with scissors, if necessary.

The Continental Clip

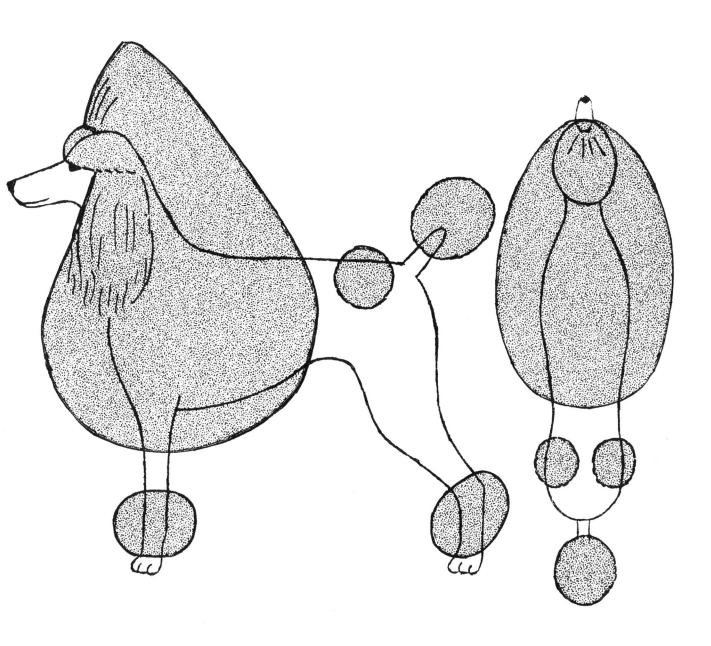

THE POODLE STANDARD states that *"in the 'Continental' clip, the face, throat, feet and base of the tail are shaved. The hindquarters are shaved with pompons (optional) on the hips. The legs are shaved, leaving bracelets on the hind legs and puffs on the forelegs. There is a pompon on the end of the tail. The entire shaven foot and a portion of the shaven foreleg above the puff are visible. The rest of the body is left in full coat but may be shaped in order to insure overall balance."*

Correct brushing and coat care are an important part of show grooming. Be sure to study thoroughly the advice offered in *Coat Care for the Show Poodle*.

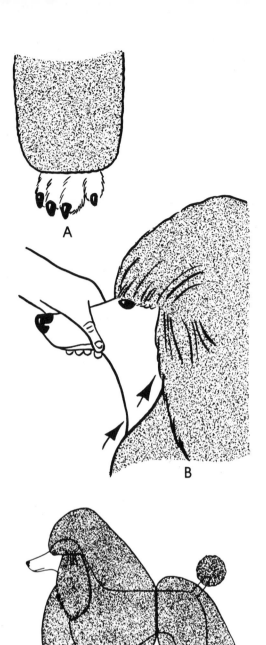

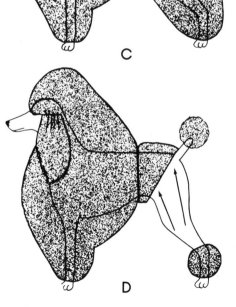

1. Follow instructions for clipping the feet. Clip only to the end of each foot (**A**) and don't expose any part of the ankle.

2. Follow instructions for clipping the face. On the sides of the head, be sure the clipped line is straight from the outside corner of the eye to the ear.

3. Follow instructions for clipping and scissoring the tail.

4. Sit the Poodle on the grooming table, facing you, to clip the throat. It should be trimmed into a "V" shape. Start at a point at the middle of the throat, about one inch below the Adam's Apple on a Toy Poodle, about one and one-half inches on a Miniature, and about two inches on a Standard, and clip each side of the neck with a #15 blade up to the front of each ear (**B**). You may have to adjust these measurements slightly according to your Poodle's length of neck.

5. Stand the Poodle on the grooming table. The first step in the Continental Clip is to make a part completely around the dog in back of the last rib (**C**), with the end-tooth of a comb or a knitting needle. The hair in front of the part, called the "mane coat" or "ruff," will remain long (to be scissored round, later on). The hair in back of the part will be shaved off the hindquarters. It's tricky to explain exactly where on the dog's body to part the hair. It must be separated where it keeps the dog in balance, and this spot varies with the individual dog. Try making the part one-half inch in back of the last rib on a Toy Poodle, about one inch in back of the last rib on a Miniature, and about two inches in back of the last rib on a Standard. Then step back and look at the dog. If he appears out of balance, move the part forward or backward. It's often necessary to experiment a little until the dog looks right. Once the part is made, comb the long hair in front of the part upward. To protect it and keep it out of the way while you shave the hindquarters, if you are a beginner, wrap a wide strip of gauze or a ribbon around the back and tie it under the chest.

6. Study the illustration of the Poodle in Continental Clip. Notice that the hindquarters are clipped close, with a bracelet on each back leg and a rosette (optional) above each hip. Begin pattern work by shaving the back legs. Use a #15 blade. Pointing clippers upward, begin about one-half inch above the hock joint on a Toy or Miniature Poodle and about one inch on a Standard, and clip up to the hindquarters (**D**). Remove all hair on the outside and inside of the back leg. Clip the opposite leg.

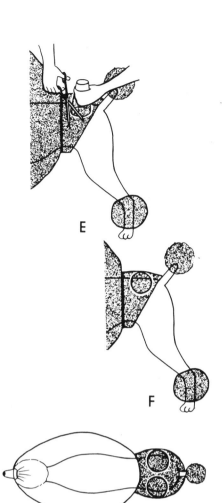

E

F

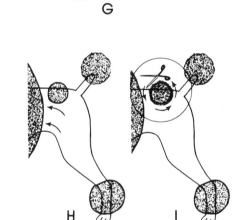

G

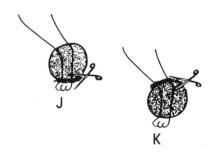

H   I

J

K

7. Use a #15 blade to clip the stomach. Pointing clippers upward, start just above the testicles or vulva and clip to the part line near the middle of the dog.

8. Clip a rosette on each side of the hindquarters. On a Toy Poodle, each rosette should be about one and one-half to two inches in diameter; on a Miniature, each rosette should be about two and one-half to three and one-half inches in diameter; and on a Standard, from three and one-half to four inches in diameter. Since it is difficult to clip round rosettes the same size and shape, use a glass or jar with an opening the size of the desired width. Hold the opening against the hair (**E**), and clip or scissor around the edge. **Sketch F** shows a side view of a rosette, round in shape, placed on the hipbone above the joint where the back leg joins the body. **Sketch G** shows a top view of the rosettes.

9. With a #15 blade, clip the remaining hair on the hindquarters, from the base of the tail, around each rosette, up to the part line near the middle of the dog (**H**).

10. Comb each rosette upward to fluff out the hair. Scissor around each one to emphasize its round shape (**I**). Then shape the tops round.

11. If rosettes are not desired, shave the hindquarters up to the part line.

12. Comb the hair below the hock joint on each back leg. Begin shaping the bracelet by combing the hair down, then scissoring around the clipped line around the foot, to remove untidy ends (**J**). Then comb the hair up and scissor off any untidy hairs above the clipped line around the leg (**K**). Comb the hair outward, then shape each bracelet with scissors. Each, when viewed from the side, is more oval than round in shape, sloping downwards from the back of the leg towards the front, emphasizing angulation. Each bracelet should be about one and one-half to two inches in diameter on a Toy, from two to three inches in diameter on a Miniature, and from three to four inches in diameter on a Standard Poodle.

13. Turn the Poodle around to stand facing you to clip the puffs on the forelegs. Begin about one and one-half to two inches above the clipped line around the foot on a Toy Poodle, two to three inches above the clipped foot line on a Miniature, and about four inches on a Standard. Clip the front and sides of each foreleg with a #15 blade up to the elbow. To take off the hair evenly, clip the back of each foreleg in the opposite direction, from the elbow down to the bracelet line. If you are a

beginner and unsure about clipping, trim the bracelet line with scissors before clipping.

14. Comb the hair on each front puff. Comb the hair down and scissor around the foot to remove any straggly hairs that fall below the clipped line. Then comb the hair up, and scissor off any untidy hairs above the clipped line around the leg. Fluff out the hair with a comb, then shape the puffs. They are more rounded in shape than the bracelets on the back legs (**L**), tapering slightly at the bottom.

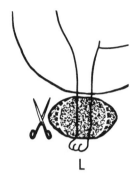

L

15. With the Poodle in a standing position on the grooming table, comb the mane coat outward for its final scissoring. Study the illustration of the Poodle in Continental Clip and notice that the long hair is shaped into a round ball. You can make shaping easier by the way you prepare the long hair. Begin by combing it upward and outward around the neck. As your hand moves backwards, comb the hair upward and slightly forward toward the head. Comb the sides of the body outward and forward. Comb the hair on the chest outward and downward, and on the underbody, downward and forward. As you scissor and shape the mane coat, think of circles and balls. Most groomers find it easier to start underneath and scissor upward, shaping the ruff round. The end result should be an overall balanced Poodle. The length of the mane coat varies with the individual dog. But be sure to trim off enough hair under the chest to show a portion of the clipped area on the forelegs between the ruff and the puffs. An excessive amount of hair under the chest or on the sides of the mane coat gives the Poodle an ungraceful look, especially when he moves about the ring.

M

16. Put up the topknot. Instructions (with sketches and photographs) for doing this are found under the English Saddle Clip. Use a comb to fan the hair upward and outward on top of the head (**M**) to blend with the rest of the coat. If the topknot is too long, it may be scissored shorter to create a better balance to the mane coat and to frame the head. Some exhibitors spray a fine mist of coat dressing or hair spray on the topknot too keep the hair in place. If you wish to do this before entering the ring, never overspray with gummy lacquers that stiffen and alter the natural coat texture.

17. Brush the ear feathering downward. Tip uneven ends with scissors if necessary.

Five Pet Variations of the Show Clips

THE HOLLYWOOD CLIP

Also Called: **THE BABY DOLL**
THE SHAWL
THE SWEETHEART BOLERO
MODIFIED ENGLISH SADDLE

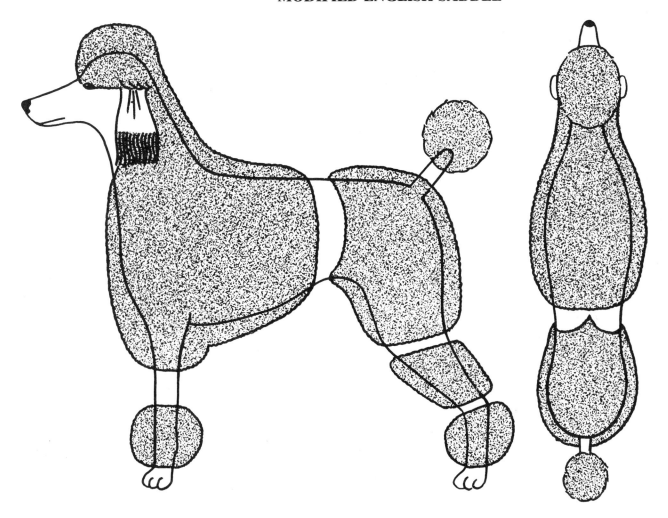

THE HOLLYWOOD CLIP is the pet variation of the English Saddle Clip. This variation was first used by Poodle owners who wanted the saddle clip, but could not cope with the coat care necessary to maintain the long hair of the ruff. The clipper work for the Hollywood Clip is done exactly the same as for the traditional English Saddle Clip. Turn back to the traditional English Saddle Clip and follow instructions for clipping the feet, face, tail, neck, stomach, bracelets and crescent-shaped saddle. The difference in this variation is only in the scissoring. Scissor the hair the same length all over, instead of leaving the long ruff. Since this is a pet variation and not acceptable in the breed ring, the hair may be any length you prefer. Toy Poodles look best with about one to one and one-half inches of hair all over. Miniature Poodles look best with about two or two and one-half inches of hair all over, and Standard Poodles look best with about three inches of hair all over. Select any ear style and topknot shape for this clip.

THE LONDON CONTINENTAL
(A pet variation)

Also Called: **THE CONTINENTAL BOLERO**
MODIFIED CONTINENTAL
CONTINENTAL DE PARIS

CLIP the feet, face, tail and stomach following basic instructions. Clip front and back of neck. Stand the Poodle with the hindquarters facing you. Use a comb to make a circular part around the dog's middle at the last rib. Use a #10 blade on the clippers. Pointing clippers upward, start just above the hock joint and clip the hair from the inside and outside of each back leg. Continue clipping up over the hips and remove all hair from the hindquarters up to the part line around the last rib. Comb out bracelets on the back legs. Scissor each one round. Comb the jacket hair. Scissor off any hairs that fall over the clipped line around the last rib and neck to make the pattern look neat. Then shape the jacket round by scissoring the hair to the same length all over. Turn the dog around to stand facing you. Scissor the front legs into pantaloons. Select any topknot and ear style with this clip.

THE ROMAN CONTINENTAL
(A pet variation)

Also Called: **MODIFIED CONTINENTAL**

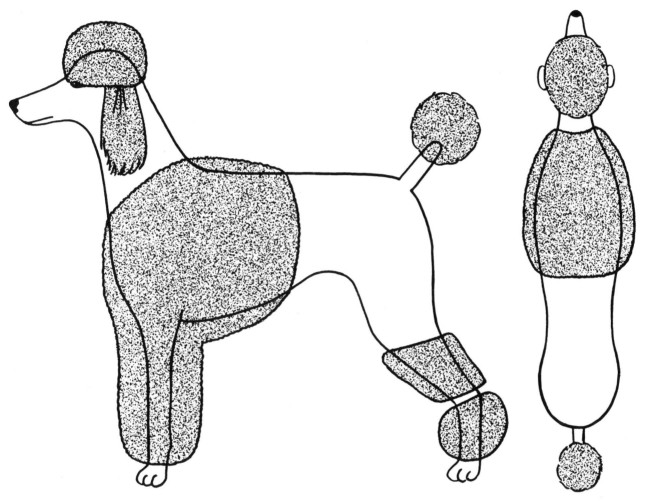

CLIP feet, face, tail and stomach following basic instructions. Clip front and back of neck. Stand the Poodle with the hindquarters facing you. Use a comb to make a circular part around the dog's middle at the last rib. Shorten a little hair in back of the part so it can easily be located later on. Use a #10 blade. Pointing clippers upward, start just above the hock joint and clip a band completely around each leg. Make this band one-half inch wide on Toys and Miniatures and about one inch wide on Standards. Move up to the stifle joint. Pointing clippers upward, clip all the hair from the upper part of each back leg and the hindquarters up to the part line around the last rib. Scissor the hair below each clipped band around the hock joint into a round bracelet. Scissor the hair below each stifle joint into a round bracelet. Comb the jacket hair. Scissor off any hairs that fall over the clipped line around the last rib and neck to make the pattern look neat. Then shape the jacket round by scissoring the hair to the same length all over. Turn the Poodle around to stand facing you. Scissor the front legs into pantaloons. Select any topknot and ear style with this clip.

THE SPANISH CONTINENTAL
(A pet variation)

Also Called: **MODIFIED CONTINENTAL**

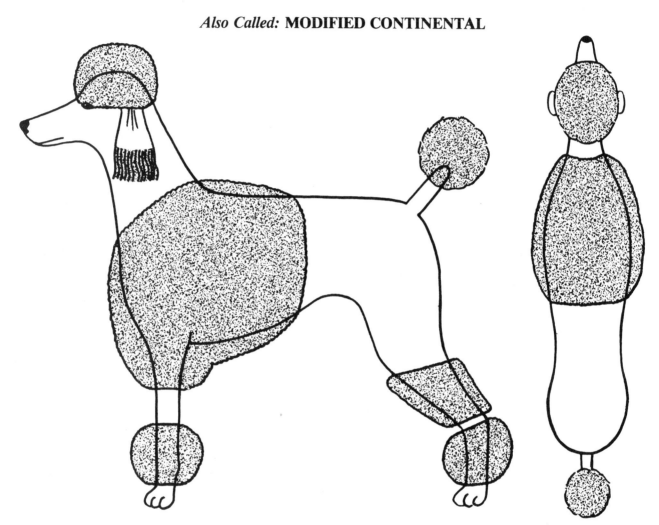

CLIP the feet, face, tail and stomach following basic instructions. Clip front and back of neck. Stand the dog with the hindquarters facing you. Use a comb to make a circular part completely around the dog at the last rib. Shorten a little hair in back of the part so it can easily be located later on. Use a #10 blade. Start just above the hock joint. Pointing clippers upward, clip a band completely around each leg. Make the band one-half inch wide on Toys and Miniatures and about one inch wide on Standards. Then move up to the stifle joint. Pointing clippers upward, clip the hair from the rest of the back legs and hindquarters up to the part line around the last rib. Scissor the hair below each clipped band around the hock joint into a round bracelet. Scissor the hair below the stifle joint on each leg into a bracelet. Comb the jacket hair. Scissor off any hairs that fall over the clipped line around the last rib and neck to make the pattern look neat. Then shape the jacket round with scissors. Turn the dog around to stand facing you. Begin one and one-half inches above the clipped ankle line on Toys, two inches above on Miniatures and three inches above on Standards, and clip each front leg up to the elbow. Shape the front bracelets round. Select any topknot and ear style with this clip.

THE PARISIAN CONTINENTAL
(A pet variation)

Also Called: **MODIFIED CONTINENTAL**

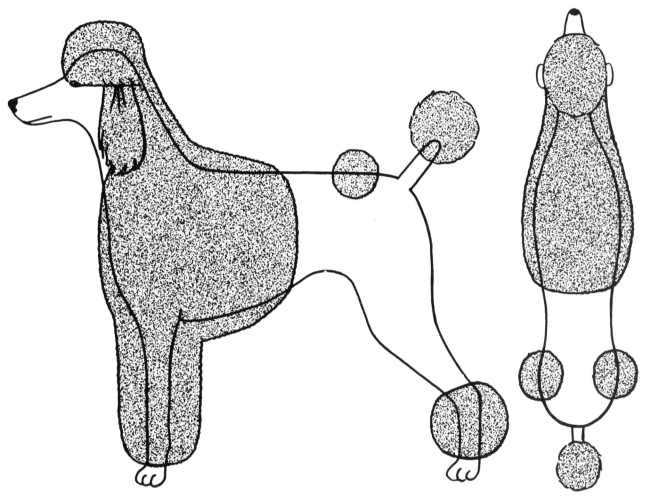

CLIP feet, face, tail and stomach following basic instructions. Clip the front of the neck. Stand the dog with the hindquarters facing you. Use a comb to make a circular part around the dog at the last rib. Shorten a little hair in back of the part so it can easily be located later. Use a #10 blade to clip the back legs. Start about one-half inch above the hock joint on Toys, three-fourths of an inch above the hock joint on Miniatures, and one inch above the hock joint on Standards. Clip up to the hindquarters, removing all hair from the inside and outside of each back leg. Clip a rosette on each side of the hindquarters. Detailed instructions for making rosettes can be found in Step 9 of the Continental Clip. Then clip the remaining hair on the hindquarters around each rosette up to the part line at the last rib. Shape a round bracelet on each back leg. Comb the body hair. Scissor off any hair that falls over the clipped line around the last rib. Then scissor the body and back of the neck to the preferred hair length. Turn the dog around to stand facing you. Shape each front leg into a pantaloon. Select any topknot and ear style with this clip. The Parisian Continental looks best with a French Moustache.

Introduction to the "Pet" Poodle Trims

THE STYLES AND PATTERNS in the following sections are called "pet" trims because they are unacceptable in the conformation show ring with one exception. The Poodle Standard states that "in the Stud Dog and Brood Bitch classes and in a noncompetitive Parade of Champions, Poodles may be shown in the Sporting Clip."

The easy-to-do clips, such as the Kennel, Sporting, Lamb, Miami, Summer Miami, Panda (or Teddy Bear), and Mink Collar precede the patterns that require more intricate body clipping, such as the New Yorker, Dutch, Sweetheart, Bandero, Diamond, Mink Collar and their variations. Throughout the pattern instructions, the shape of the hind legs is called a "pantaloon." They are scissored rather full in shape, but the outline follows the Poodle's natural conformation, showing angulation above the hock joint and the curve of the stifle joint. Even though the sketches show a full, almost straight hind leg, do remember to emphasize angulation, as seen in the photograph below.

The Leg Variations

The following five leg variations may be used with any body pattern in place of the full or "pantaloon" leg style described in the following clipping sections. The different leg variations are also pictured after most of the body patterns.

The Bell Bottom Variation

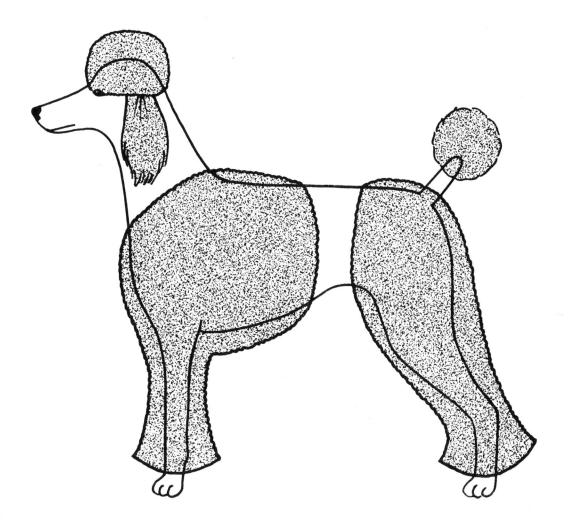

Clip the Poodle's feet, face, tail, stomach, neck, and the selected body pattern. Clip or scissor the body hair following the pattern instructions.

Stand the dog on the grooming table with hindquarters facing you. The bell bottom leg is achieved with scissors, but preliminary combing of the leg hair is most important. Comb the hair outward from the leg. Do not comb upward, for you will not be able to scissor the shape of a "bell." Begin scissoring at the hip, following the natural curve of the leg at the stifle joint, as shown in the illustration. At the hock joint, gradually increase the length of the hair until you reach the points of the "bell" at the ankle. Comb the hair downward and outward into a bell shape as you scissor near the ankle. Keep combing and scissoring until you create the desired shape. Scissor all four legs and make them even. This style requires expert scissoring. Don't be discouraged if you do not get the proper shape the first time you try. Practice makes perfect!

97

The Bolero Leg Variation

Clip the Poodle's feet, face, tail, stomach, neck and the selected body pattern. Scissor the body hair following the pattern instructions.

Stand the dog on the grooming table with hindquarters facing you. Comb out the leg hair. At the hock joint, point clippers upward, using a #15 or any of the narrow cutting blades, and clip a narrow strip around the leg. Make the band about one-quarter inch wide on Toy Poodles, about one-half inch wide on Miniatures, and about one inch wide on Standards. Scissor the hair below each clipped band into a bracelet. Comb out the hair above each clipped band. Scissor off any hairs that fall below the clipped strip, then shape the rest of the leg into the pantaloon style, following the dog's natural conformation, and emphasizing the curve of the stifle joint.

Turn the dog around to stand facing you. Notice on the illustration that the clipped bands and bracelets on the front legs are lined up evenly with those on the back legs. To avoid making a mistake, use chalk or scissors to mark the hair at the spot where you want to begin clipping. Point clippers upward and clip a band of corresponding size completely around each front leg. Scissor the front bracelets, making them even in size and shape with the back bracelets. Comb the hair above the clipped bands and scissor each into a pantaloon shape.

The Fifth Avenue Leg Variation

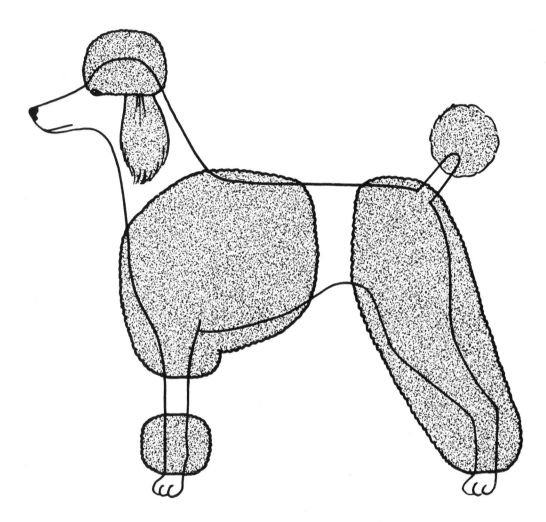

Clip the Poodle's feet, face, tail, stomach, neck, and the selected body pattern. Scissor the body hair following pattern instructions.

Stand the dog on the grooming table with hindquarters facing you. Comb the hair on the back legs upward and outward to fluff the coat. Scissor each back leg into a pantaloon shape, following the dog's natural conformation, emphasizing angulation above the hock joint and at the curve of the stifle joint.

Turn the dog around to stand facing you. In this variation, a bracelet is trimmed on each front leg. Start about one and one-half inches above the clipped line around the ankle on Toy Poodles, about two to three inches on Miniatures, and about three to four inches on Standards. Clip the front and sides of each front leg up to the elbow with a #15 blade. To take off the hair evenly, clip the back of each front leg in the opposite direction, from the elbow down to the bracelet line with the same blade. Comb out the bracelets and scissor each one to a round shape. Comb the hair downward on the front of the chest near the elbows, then scissor any straggly ends that fall below the clipped lines to make the pattern look neat.

The Miami Leg Variation

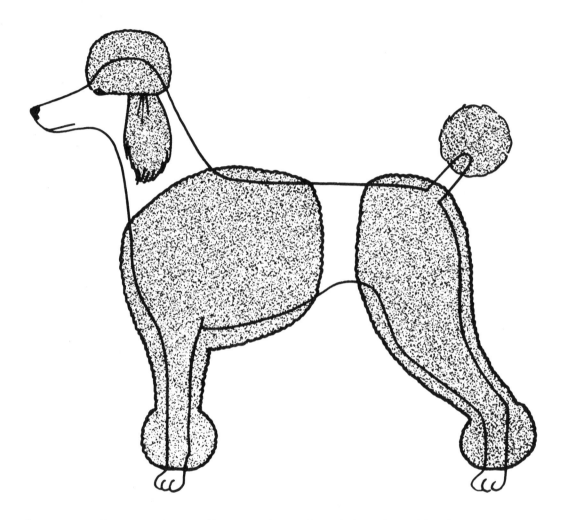

Clip the Poodle's feet, face, tail, stomach, neck and the selected body pattern. Regardless of which pattern you choose, the body hair must always be trimmed short when you use the Miami leg variation, to blend in with the shorter leg hair.

Stand the Poodle on the grooming table with hindquarters facing you. Comb out the back legs. Clip with a #4 or #5 blade, or scissor (to a length of about one-half inch) the inside and out-side of each back leg down to the hock joint. The hair below each hock joint is shaped into a bracelet. Begin by combing the hair downward toward the foot, then scissor off any untidy ends that fall below the clipped line around the ankle. Comb the bracelet up and scissor the uneven hairs that extend above the clipped line around the hock joint. Fluff out the hair with your comb. Shape each bracelet with scissors to a length of about one and one-half to two inches in diameter on Toy Poodles, two to three inches in diameter on Miniatures and three to four inches in diameter on Standards. Make the back bracelets even in size and shape.

Turn the Poodle around to stand facing you. Comb out the front legs. To line up front bracelets evenly with those on the back legs, scissor a spot in the hair where each bracelet will begin. Then clip or scissor each front leg to a length of about one-half inch down to the bracelet line. Scissor each front bracelet even in size and shape with those on the back legs.

100

The Saddle Leg Variation

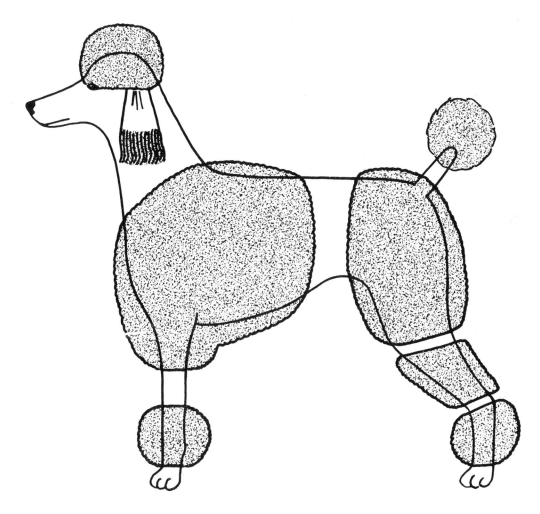

Clip the Poodle's feet, face, tail, stomach, neck, and the selected body pattern. Stand the Poodle on the grooming table with hindquarters facing you. Use a #15 or any of the narrow cutting blades, point clippers upward at the hock joint and clip a narrow band completely around each leg. Make the clipped strip about one-fourth inch wide on Toy Poodles, about one-half inch wide on Miniatures and about one inch wide on Standards. The hair below the clipped band is scissored into a bracelet on each leg.

Start at the center bone of the stifle joint. Point clippers upward and clip another band of the same width completely around each leg. The hair below this band is scissored into a bracelet on each leg. Scissor the hindquarters, back, ribs and chest hair as described in the pattern instructions.

Turn the dog around to stand facing you. Start about one and one-half inches above the clipped ankle line on Toys, about two to three inches on Miniatures, and about three to four inches on Standards, and clip the front and sides of each foreleg up to the elbow. To take off the hair evenly, clip the back of each foreleg in the opposite direction, from the elbow down to the bracelet line. The hair below the clipped area on each front leg is scissored into a bracelet. Comb the hair downward on the chest near the elbows and trim off any untidy ends that fall below the clipped lines.

The Sporting (or Kennel) Clip

Also Called: **THE UTILITY CLIP**
THE MODIFIED LAMB CLIP

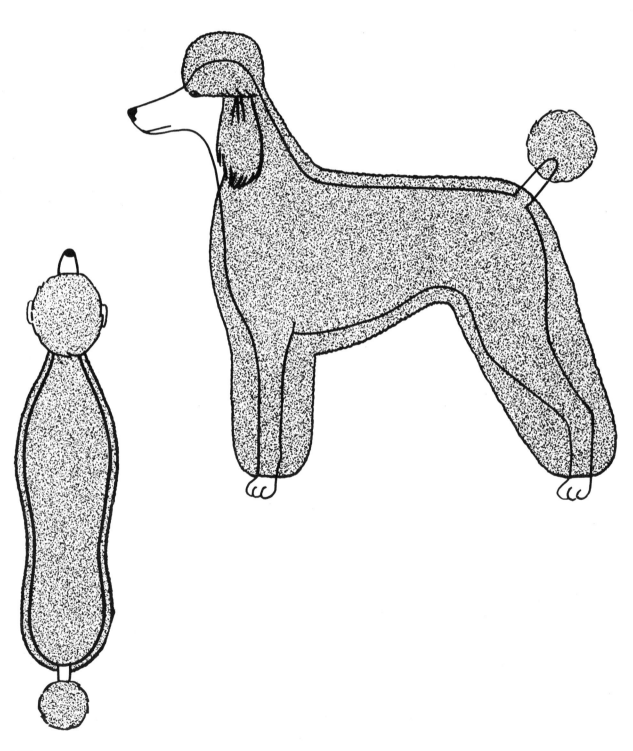

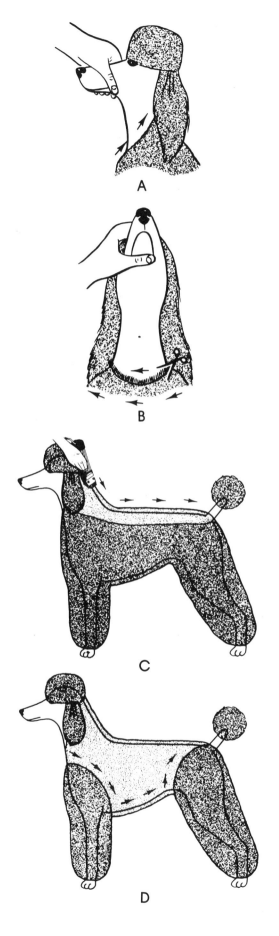

A

B

C

D

1. Follow instructions for clipping the feet.
2. Follow instructions for clipping the face. The face may be clipped clean or you may select any moustache style.
3. Follow instructions for clipping and scissoring the tail.
4. Follow instructions for clipping the stomach. Clip up to the last rib.
5. Sit the dog on the grooming table, facing you. Clip the front of the neck with a #10 blade. Start about one inch below the Adam's apple on Toy Poodles, two inches below on Miniatures, and three inches below on Standards. Pointing clippers upward, clip to the front of each ear (**A**). The hair below the Adam's apple may be trimmed into a "V" or rounded slightly (**B**). When the neck is clipped, comb the hair at the clipped line upward, then scissor off any hair that extends above the line to make the pattern look neat.
6. Stand the Poodle on the grooming table. Use a #4 or #5 blade to clip the body. The hair on the back of the neck and body is clipped off to an even length of from one-half inch to one inch depending on the blade you use. Start at the base of the skull and clip the hair from the back and sides of the neck. Then clip down the middle of the back to the base of the tail (**C**). Using the clippers in this direction, clip off all the hair on top of the body. Do not use the clippers below the shoulders and hips. Clip around these areas (**D**). Clip the hair between the shoulders and hips on each side of the dog. Clip the hair under the chest from in back of the front legs to the last rib. When you have finished clipping, the hair will be from one-half to one inch in length all over the body, with the exception of the hair on the shoulders and hips. This long hair remaining on the shoulders and hips will be used for blending when the legs are scissored.
7. Stand the dog with the hindquarters facing you. Comb the hair on the back legs in an upward and outward motion to fluff the coat. The leg is shaped in the popular pantaloon style, but following the Poodle's natural conformation, to show angulation above the hock joint and the curve of the stifle joint. Depending on the length and texture of your dog's coat, you may scissor the leg as full or as tapered as you wish. Begin

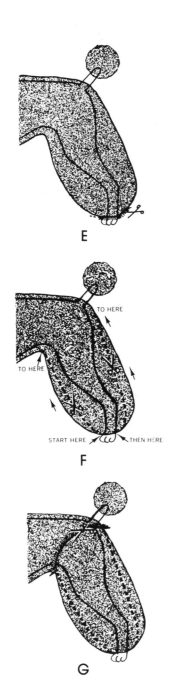

E

F

G

by scissoring any straggly hairs that fall below the clipped line around the ankle (**E**). Then shape the leg. Start at the ankle and work up to the hip. When one part of the leg is scissored, begin again at the ankle and scissor another part up to the hips. Work completely around the leg in this manner (**F**), leaving the same amount of hair on each side of the leg. Hold the scissors flat against the hair you are working on, to take a little hair off at a time. If you are not satisfied with your results, comb the hair again, then re-scissor the same area. When you reach the hip, start blending the leg hair with the short body hair. Comb the hair above the hips upward and gradually shorten by scissoring to blend with the body hair (**G**). Keep combing upward and scissoring the hair short, until the line from the hindquarters over the hips is smooth. Scissor the other back leg. Make it the same size and shape as the opposite leg. Be sure the hair on each side of the hindquarters is blended evenly.

8. Turn the dog around to stand facing you. Comb the hair on the front legs up and out. Scissor the front legs, making them even in size with the back legs. Comb the hair at the shoulders upward. Blend this hair with the short body hair exactly as you did over the hips, by combing the hair up and scissoring until the line from the body to the shoulders is smooth and sleek. Comb the hair on the chest and between the front legs. Scissor this hair to the same length as the shoulder and body hair.

9. Sit the Poodle on the grooming table, facing you. Comb the topknot hair upward and forward. Scissor a round or square topknot. When working at the base of the skull, remember to blend the topknot hair with the short hair on the neck.

10. Comb the hair on the ears. Select any ear style for the Sporting Clip.

    NOTE: If you wish to leave more than one inch of body hair on a thin Poodle, use scissors instead of a clipper blade to do the body work. Comb the body hair up and forward to fluff the coat, then evenly scissor the hair to the desired length on the back, ribs, chest and neck, up to the base of the skull where the topknot begins.
    For another variation of the Sporting Clip—use the Bell-Bottom Leg Style.

The Town and Country Clip

Also Called: **THE RIVIERA**
THE COWBOY
THE SPORTSMAN
THE SWISS CLIP

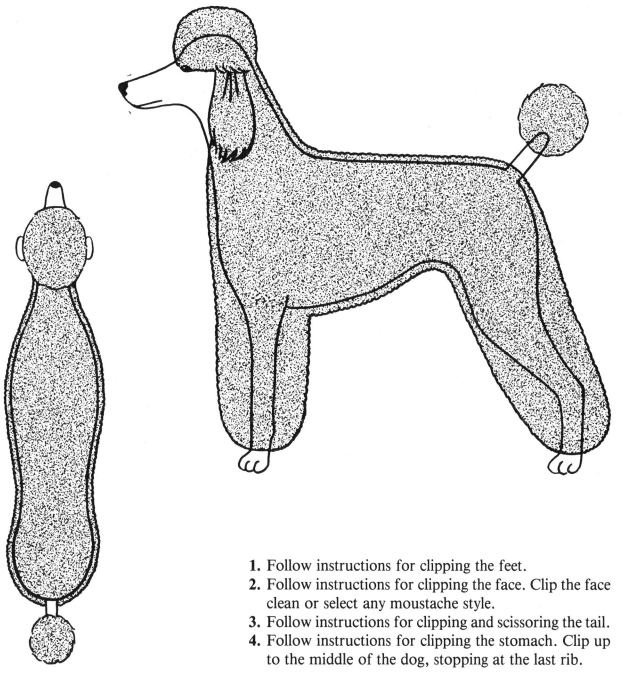

1. Follow instructions for clipping the feet.
2. Follow instructions for clipping the face. Clip the face clean or select any moustache style.
3. Follow instructions for clipping and scissoring the tail.
4. Follow instructions for clipping the stomach. Clip up to the middle of the dog, stopping at the last rib.

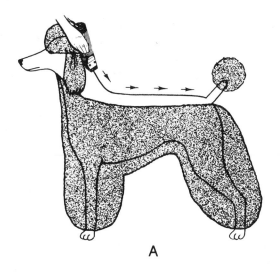

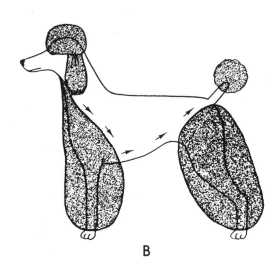

A

B

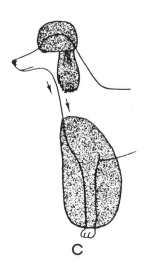

C

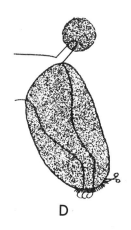

D

5. Stand the dog on the grooming table. Use a #10 blade to clip the body. Do all body clipping by using the clippers with the growth of hair, from the head to the tail. Do not turn the clippers the opposite way or the body will appear skinned. Start at the base of the skull and clip the hair from the back of the neck. Continue clipping straight down the back to the base of the tail (**A**). Clip off all hair on top of the body, but do not use the clippers below the shoulders or hips. Clip around these areas (**B**). The long hair remaining on each shoulder and hip will be used for blending when the legs are scissored. Clip the hair on the ribs between the shoulders and hips. Clip under the chest from the back of the front legs to the last rib. When you have finished clipping the body, the hair will be short with the exception of a tuft of long hair on each shoulder and hip.

6. Clip the sides of the neck with the #10 blade. Start under each ear and clip down to a line even with the breast bone (**C**). Clip the front of the neck with the #10 blade from the throat down to the breast bone. Leave this hair long for the moment, to be scissored later when the shoulders and front legs are shaped.

7. Stand the Poodle on the grooming table with his hindquarters facing you. Comb the hair on the back legs up and out. The leg shape for the Town & Country is a full pantaloon shape, but following the dog's natural conformation to show angulation at the hock joint and the curve of the stifle joint. Scissor off any hairs that fall below the clipped line around the ankle (**D**). Then

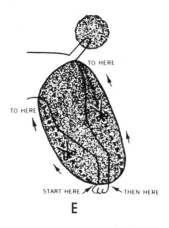

E

F

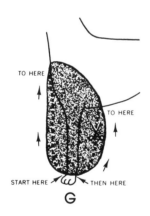

G

H

begin shaping the leg. The fastest and easiest way to shape the leg is to begin scissoring at the ankle and work up to the hip, stopping at the point where the leg joins the body. Scissor one part of the leg from the ankle up to the hip; then begin again at the ankle, and scissor another part up to the hip. Work completely around the leg (**E**), until you have the desired shape. The hair should be the same length on each side of the leg. If you have difficulty in scissoring the inside of the leg, lift the opposite leg with your free hand. Always hold the scissors flat against the hair you are working on. Do not dig into the coat with the scissor points. If you are not satisfied with the leg shape, recomb the part you are working on and begin again. When the leg is completely scissored up to the hip, start to shorten the hair to blend with the body hair. Comb the leg hair up, then gradually scissor the hair shorter as you work from the hip up to the hindquarters as shown in (**F**). Keep combing the hair up and scissoring the hair until the line from the hindquarters down over the hips is smooth. Scissor the opposite leg. Be sure the back legs are even in size and shape and blended evenly at the hip line.

8. Turn the Poodle around to stand facing you. Comb the hair on the front legs up and out. Scissor off any hairs that fall below the clipped line around the ankle. Then begin shaping the leg. Start at the ankle and scissor one part of the leg up to the elbow. Do this completely around the leg (**G**), until you have the desired shape. When the leg is scissored up to the elbow, comb the hair on the front of the chest and shoulders. Gradually scissor this hair short to blend with the body hair as you work from the elbow up to the shoulders (**H**). Keep combing the hair up and scissoring until the line over the shoulders and front of the chest is smooth. Scissor the hair between the front legs to blend with the short body hair. Scissor the opposite front leg and shoulder.

9. Select a round or square-shaped topknot.

10. Select any ear style with the Town and Country Clip.

THE BELL-BOTTOM TOWN AND COUNTRY CLIP
(A variation)

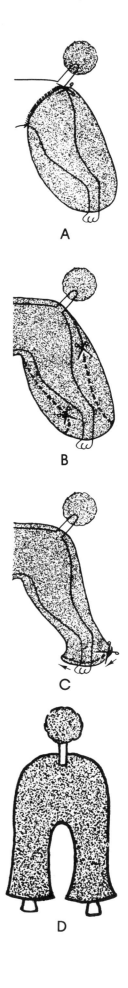

This is a variation of the Town & Country with a different leg shape. Use the bell-bottom leg style only on Poodles with profuse coats. Do not consider this style for puppies or for adult dogs with soft coats.

Clip the feet, face, tail, stomach and body as instructed in the Town and Country Clip. Stand the dog with his hindquarters facing you, to scissor the back legs. Begin working at the hips, just above the point where the leg joins the body. Comb this hair up. With scissors, work up to the hindquarters, gradually shortening the long hair on the hips to blend with the short body hair (**A**). Keep combing the hair up and scissoring the long hair short, until the line from the hindquarters down over the hips is smooth. To shape the rest of the leg in the bell-bottom style, the combing of hair is important. Comb the leg hair out, not up. Begin scissoring the leg below the hip and work down to and around the stifle joint, following the natural curve of the leg (**B**). At the hock joint, gradually increase the hair length. Comb the hair down and out below the hock joint, and scissor the points of the bell (**C**). Scissor the other back leg. The correct back view of the rear legs is shown in (**D**). Turn the Poodle around to stand facing you. Start just above the point where the front leg joins the body. Comb this hair up. With scissors, work up to the shoulders and gradually shorten the long hair to blend with the short body hair as you did on the hindquarters. Comb the hair on the chest up and scissor to the same length as the shoulder hair. Comb the hair on the front legs out, not up. Scissor each front leg into the bell shape. Select any topknot or ear style with this clip.

108

The Lamb Clip

Also Called: **THE ASTRAKAN**
THE KARAKUL
THE RETRIEVER
THE CURLY CLIP

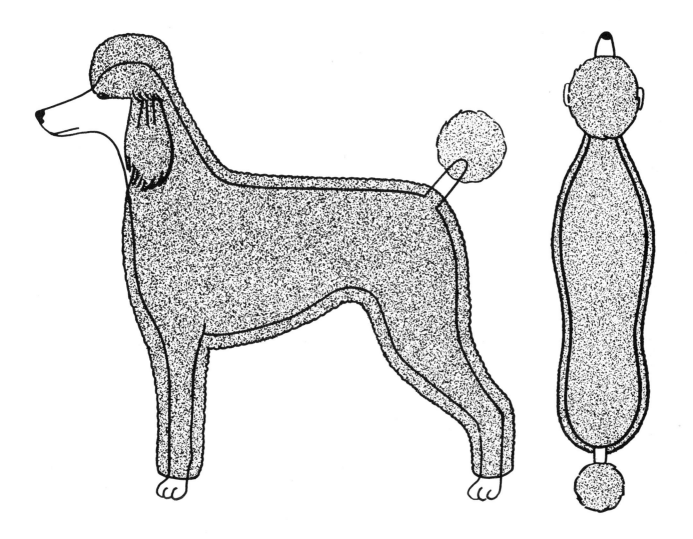

1. Follow instructions for clipping the feet.
2. Follow instructions for clipping the face. Clip the face clean or select any moustache style.
3. Follow instructions for clipping and scissoring the tail.
4. Clip the stomach with a #10 blade. Clip up to the middle of the dog, stopping at the last rib.
5. Sit the dog on the grooming table, facing you. Use a #10 blade. Clip the front of the neck. Start at a point about one inch below the Adam's apple on Toy Poo-

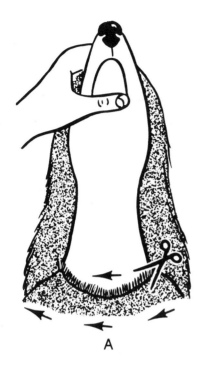

dles, about two inches below on Miniatures and about three inches below on Standards. Pointing clippers upward, clip off all hair on the throat and underside of muzzle. The clipped line around the front of the neck is rounded (**A**). When clipper work is finished, comb the hair upward and scissor off any hair that extends over the clipped line to make the pattern look neat.

6. You are ready to do body work. Study the illustration of this clip and notice that the hair is an even length on the body and legs. To get this "lamb" look, you must do the body with scissors, not clippers. If you are clipping a Toy Poodle, the body and leg hair should be from one-half inch to one inch long; on a Miniature Poodle, the hair should be about one to two inches long; and on a Standard Poodle, about two to three inches long. Comb out the body hair. Use the comb in an upward motion to lift the hair rather than flatten it. Stand the Poodle with his hindquarters facing you. Begin body work by scissoring the hindquarters. Shape the hindquarters round and follow the natural contours of the body as you scissor over the hips, back, ribs, chest, shoulders and sides of the neck, up to the point where the topknot begins at the base of the skull. Scissor off a little hair at a time, holding the scissors flat against the hair you are working on. The most important point about the Lamb Clip is to make the hair an even length. The easiest way to evenly scissor the body is to do the Poodle's right side with his hindquarters facing you. Then scissor the front of the chest and turn the Poodle around to face you and scissor the left side of his body.

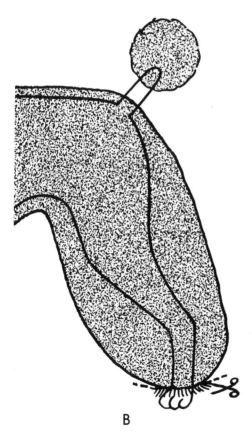

A

B

7. Study the illustration of the Lamb Clip again. Because the leg hair is the same length as the body hair, the shape follows the natural contour of the leg. Stand the dog on the table with his hindquarters facing you. Comb the hair on the back legs up and out. Begin scissoring by removing any straggly hairs that fall below the clipped line around the ankle (**B**). Begin again at the ankle and shape the leg as in (**C**). Because you leave the same amount of hair all over, your scissoring will follow the natural curve of the leg, showing the angulation above the hock bone and the curve of the stifle. Scissor each back leg even in size and shape.

8. Turn the dog around to stand facing you. Comb the hair on the front legs up and out. Begin scissoring by removing any straggly hairs that fall below the clipped

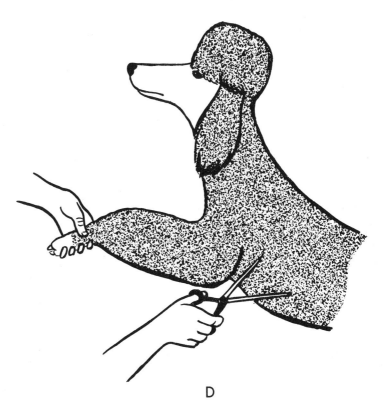

D

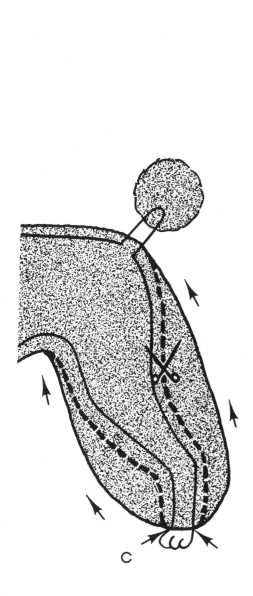

C

line around the ankles. Scissor the front legs, leaving the same amount of hair as you did on the back legs. When scissoring where the front legs meet the chest, comb the hair up and scissor until the hair is an even length. To scissor the hair on the chest under the front legs, lift the leg under which you want to scissor. Pull it slightly forward (**D**), to avoid cutting holes in the coat.

10. Sit the Poodle on the grooming table, facing you. Select a round or square topknot. The ears may be clipped in any style or left full.

TERRIER LAMB VARIATION

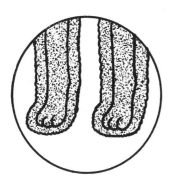

The Terrier Lamb Clip is done the same as the regular Lamb Clip with two exceptions. Do not clip the feet or the tail. Clip the face, stomach and neck. Scissor the body and legs are instructed above, leaving the same length of hair all over. Instead of clipping the feet with clippers, comb the hair over the paws and neatly trim them by scissoring around the edges of the toes. Do not remove hair in between the toes. Do not clip the tail. Scissor the tail, without leaving a pompon at the end, to the same length as the body hair.

111

The Mandarin Clip

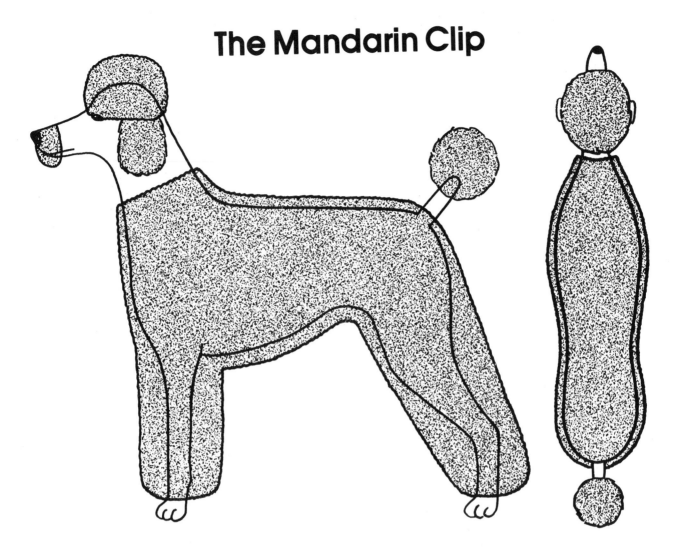

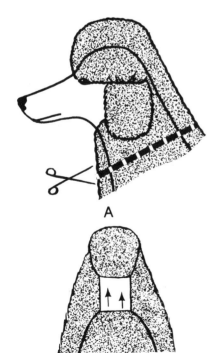

A

B

1. Follow instructions for clipping the feet.
2. Follow instructions for clipping the face. Clip the face clean or select any moustache style.
3. Follow instructions for clipping and scissoring the tail.
4. Clip the stomach with a #10 blade. Clip up to the middle of the dog, stopping at the last rib.
5. Sit the Poodle on the grooming table facing you to clip the Mandarin collar. Study the large illustration of the Mandarin Clip above. Notice that the collar line completely encircles the neck, about half-way between the base of the skull and withers in back, and half-way between the throat and breast bone in front. Before using clippers, cut the collar line around the neck with scissors to avoid making a mistake (A). Then use a #10 blade. Start clipping the back of the neck first. Pointing clippers upward, clip from the collar line to the base of the skull (B). Clip each side of the neck from the collar line up to the base of the ear. Clip the front of the neck from the collar line up to the throat (C).

C

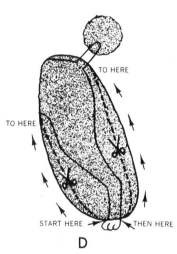

D

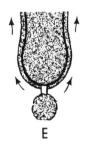

E

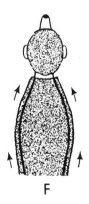

F

6. Stand the dog with the hindquarters facing you. Comb the hair on the back legs up and out to fluff the coat. The legs should be scissored into a full pantaloon shape. First, scissor off any hairs that fall below the clipped line around the ankle. Then begin shaping the leg. The easiest way to shape a pantaloon is to begin scissoring at the ankle and work up to the hip, stopping at the point where the leg joins the body. Scissor on part of the leg from the ankle up to the hip; then begin again at the ankle, and scissor another part up to the hip. Work completely around the leg (**D**) until you have the desired shape, but always follow the Poodle's natural conformation to show angulation above the hock joint and the curve of the stifle joint. Always hold the scissors flat against the hair you are working on. Never dig into the coat with the scissor points. Scissor the opposite leg. Be sure both back legs are even in size and shape.

7. Comb the hair on the hips and hindquarters. Continue scissoring up from the legs on each side, rounding the hindquarters (**E**). Comb out the body hair. Continue scissoring over the hips, back, ribs, chest and shoulders, leaving the same amount of hair all over and following the natural contours of the dog's body (**F**). Scissor the hair under the chest to the same length as on top.

8 Scissor the hair above the withers, the Mandarin collar, to the same length as the body hair. When working near the clipped line around the neck, comb the hair upward and forward, then scissor off any hairs that extend above the clipped line to make the Mandarin collar look neat.

9. Turn the dog around to stand facing you. Comb the hair on the front legs. Scissor off any hairs that fall below the clipped line around the ankles. Then shape each front leg into a full pantaloon. Start at the ankle and scissor one part of the leg up to the elbow. Begin again at the ankle and scissor another part of the leg up to the elbow. Work completely around the leg until you have the desired shape. Scissor the other front leg. Make both front legs even in size and shape.

10. Select any topknot style with the Mandarin Clip.

11. Select any ear style.

NOTE: *For five variations of the Mandarin Clip, use the Bolero, Bell-Bottom, Fifth Avenue, Miami and Saddle leg styles.*

The Miami Clip

Also Called: **THE PALM SPRINGS**
THE CLOWN
THE PONJOLA
THE STRIPPER
THE BALLERINA

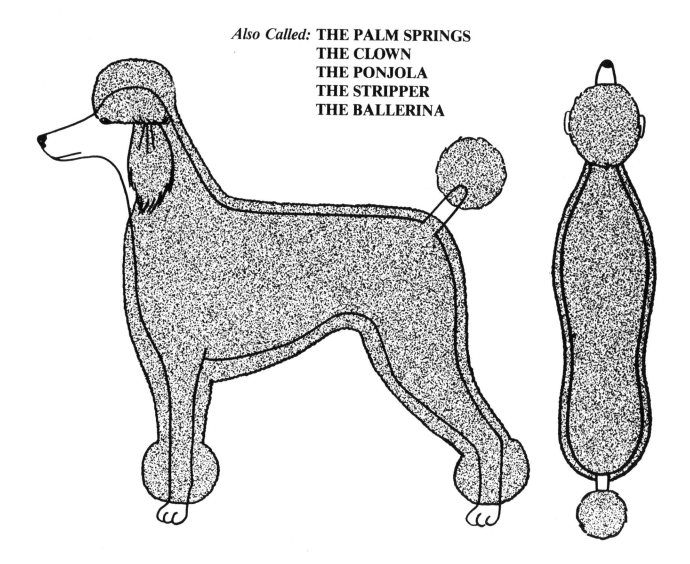

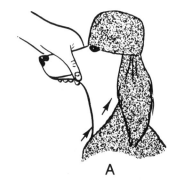

1. Follow instructions for clipping the feet.
2. Follow instructions for clipping the face. Clip the face clean or select any moustache style.
3. Follow instructions for clipping and scissoring the tail.
4. Follow instructions for clipping the stomach. Clip up to the middle of the dog, stopping at the last rib.
5. Clip the front of the neck. Sit the Poodle on the grooming table, facing you. Use a #10 blade. Start about one inch below the Adam's apple on a Toy Poodle, about two inches below on a Miniature, and about 3 inches below on a Standard. Pointing clippers upward, clip to the front of each ear. The part of the neck below the Adam's apple is rounded slightly with the clippers (**A**).
6. Stand the dog on the grooming table. Use a #4 or #5 blade to clip the body. Starting at the base of the skull,

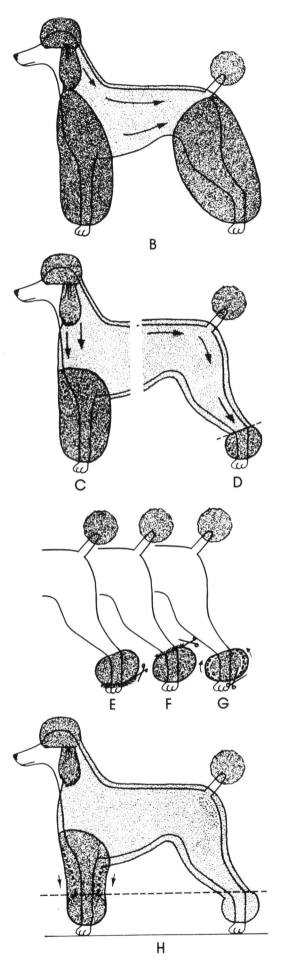

work down to the tail and clip off all hair on the neck, shoulders, back, ribs, hips, and under the chest (**B**). Use the clippers in one direction.

7. Start under each ear and clip down with the #4 or #5 blade. Clean off all hair on the sides of the neck and chest (**C**).

8. Stand the Poodle on the grooming table with his hindquarters facing you. With the #4 or #5 blade, start at the hips and clip the top and underside of each back leg down to the hock joint (**D**). Do not clip below the hock joint.

9. The hair below the hock joint on each back leg is scissored into a bracelet. Comb the hair down toward the foot and scissor the untidy ends that fall below the clipped line around the ankle (**E**). Then comb the bracelet up and scissor the uneven hairs that extend above the clipped line around the hock joint (**F**). Fluff out the hair with a comb. Scissor each bracelet into round shape (**G**). Each bracelet should be about one and one-half to two inches in diameter on a Toy Poodle, two to three inches in diameter on a Miniature Poodle, and three to four inches in diameter on a Standard Poodle. Because so much body and leg hair is clipped off, make the bracelets as full as possible. The back bracelets must be even in size and shape.

10. Turn the Poodle to stand facing you. The most difficult part of the Miami Clip is setting the bracelets on the front legs. The front bracelets must be evenly lined-up with the back bracelets. If they are higher or lower, the clip will look wrong when the dog walks. Before clipping, use chalk to mark the spot on each leg where you want the bracelet to begin. Then clip the front legs with the #4 or #5 blade from the shoulders down to this line (**H**). Clean off any remaining hair on the shoulders or underside of the chest with the blade.

11. Shape the front bracelets. Comb the bracelet down toward the foot and scissor the untidy ends that fall below the clipped line around the ankle. Then comb the bracelet up, and scissor the uneven hairs that extend above the clipped line around the leg. Fluff out the hair with a comb. Scissor each front bracelet into a round shape exactly as you did on the back legs. The bracelets must be even in size and shape on all four legs.

12. Sit the Poodle on the grooming table, facing you. Comb and fluff the topknot hair upward and forward. Scissor a round or square-shaped topknot. Select any ear style with this clip.

How To Shape Bracelets

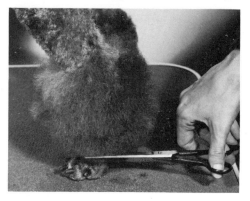

Begin by combing the hair downward towards the foot. Scissor off any untidy ends that fall below the clipped line around the Poodle's foot.

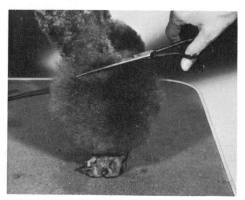

Comb the hair upward, then scissor off the uneven hairs that extend above the clipped line around the hock joint.

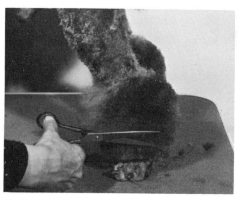

Fluff the bracelet outward with a comb. Shape the bracelet with scissors.

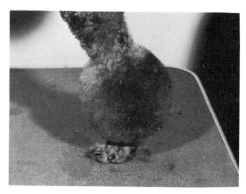

The finished bracelet.

116

THE SUMMER MIAMI

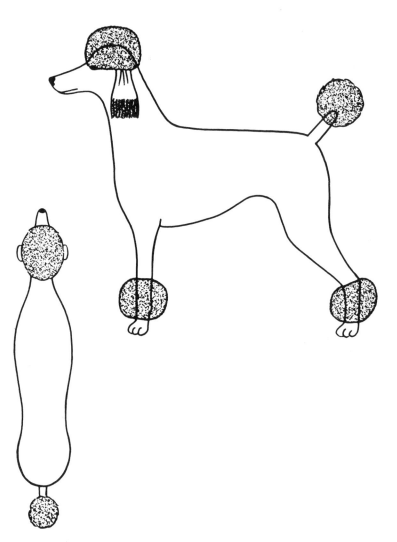

An excellent hot weather clip which can also be used for badly matted Poodles that must be clipped short for coat restoration. This variation of the Miami Clip differs only in the length of body and leg hair. Refer back to the Miami Clip where instructed.

1—5. Follow preceding instructions.
  6. Follow preceding instructions but use a #10 blade instead of a #4 or #5.
  7. Follow preceding instructions but use a #10 blade instead of a #4 or #5.
  8. Follow preceding instructions but use a #10 blade instead of #4 or #5.
  9. Follow preceding instructions.
10. Follow preceding instructions but use a #10 blade instead of #4 or #5.
11. Follow preceding instructions.
12. Follow preceding instructions.

The Panda (or Teddy Bear) Clip

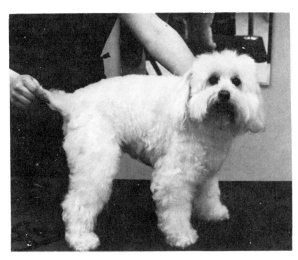

The Panda (or Teddy Bear) clip is a good choice for this Cocker-Poodle cross breed. While he does not distinctly resemble either breed, his coat is more Poodle-like, but of soft texture, especially around the head.

The dog with its body and legs trimmed. The hindquarters have been shaped with scissors to show the dog's natural angulation above the hock and at the curve of the stifle joint. The head area is scissored last.

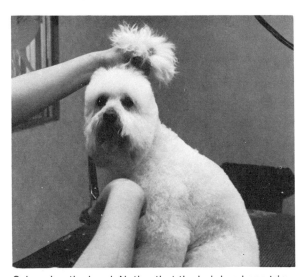

Scissoring the head. Notice that the hair has been trimmed short at the stop and the inside corners of each eye. It increases gradually in length toward the sides of the face and the ears.

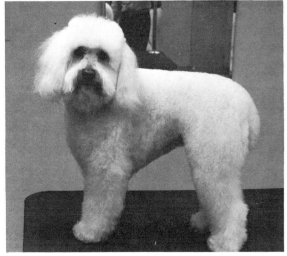

The finished Panda Clip. The tail has been scissored to an even length all over. A pompon is optional.

The Panda, or Teddy Bear, trim is an excellent style for owners who dislike Poodle trims with the feet, face and tail clipped closely. And it is perfect for the various Poodle cross-breeds (Cocker/Poodle, Schnauzer/Poodle, Shih Tzu/Poodle, for instance) that neither resemble a distinct breed and have less-than-ideal coat texture. The attractiveness of this trim is that it gives the dog a casual, yet charming, look.

1. Clip the hair from between the pads on the underside of each foot. Do not clip the tops of the feet or between the toes.

2. A tail pompon is optional. If a pompon is desired, follow instructions for clipping and scissoring the tail. If no clipping is desired, scissor the tail hair to a length of about one inch all over, with or without a pompon.

3. Follow instructions for clipping the stomach. Clip up to the middle of the dog, stopping at the last rib.

4. Stand the Poodle on the grooming table to face you. Ideally, the look you are trying to achieve is that of a neat and almost natural-looking dog, with no closely clipped areas. The hair on the front and back of the neck and the top and underside of the body is scissored or clipped to a length of about one inch. Clipping the hair to this length is best accomplished with a snap-on comb (previously mentioned in the *Equipment* chapter) that attaches over a regular clipper blade. All body clipping is done with the growth of hair, from the head to the tail. Begin at the base of the skull, and clip the hair on the back and sides of the neck.

Then clip down the middle of the back to the base of the tail. Using clippers in this direction, shorten the hair all over the body and under the chest. Clip over the hindquarters partially down onto the back legs. Gently lift up the Poodle's head and clip downward from the throat to the chest. Clip over the shoulders down to the elbows. When you have finished working with the snap-on comb or scissors, the hair should be about one inch long, with longer hair remaining only on the legs, face, and head.

5. Stand the dog on the table with hindquarters facing you. Comb the hair on the back legs outward to prepare for scissoring. Scissor neatly around one foot to remove straggly ends, then shape it round. Do not remove any hair between the toes. Shape the leg evenly all over, considering the dog's natural conformation by scissoring to show angulation above the hock joint and the curve of the stifle joint. Work completely around the leg in this manner, leaving the same amount of hair on each side. As you gradually work upward, blend the leg hair evenly into the body coat. Scissor the hair under the tail and around the anal area to blend with the body hair. Scissor the other back leg, making it even in size and shape.

6. Turn the dog around to stand facing you. Comb the hair on the front legs outward. Scissor around the feet to remove straggly hairs, then shape them round. Then scissor the front legs, making them even in size with the back legs. Be sure to blend the longer hair at the elbows into the short body hair, until the line over the shoulders and down the legs appears smooth. If any long hairs remain between the front legs, scissor them to the same length as the rest of the body.

7. Sit the dog on the grooming table to face you. All work on the head is done with scissors. Begin by combing out the facial hair. Then use blunt-tippoed scissors to trim an inverted "V" between the eyes. After the "V" is formed, shorten the hair at the inside corners of each eye with the scissors, going over the bridge of the nose and under the eyes, gradually increasing the length of hair as you scissor toward the sides of the face and the ears. Lift each ear leather, as you scissor neatly underneath, to make the ears lie close to the head when hanging in natural position. Comb the moustache and beard hair and trim it into the German moustache style as on Page 69.

8. Comb the topknot hair upward and slightly forward. Shorten the topknot in front with blunt-tipped scissors to prevent hair from falling into the eyes. Then scissor the rest of the head. On the Panda or Teddy Bear clip, the topknot follows the natural round shape of the skull, with more hair remaining in the center of the head, but tapering to the sides. The hair at the back of the skull blends into the hair on the neck. The topknot at the sides of the head blends into the ear feathering. There is no scissored or clipped separation between the topknot and the ears.

9. The ear feathering is left long and full.

The New Yorker Clip

Also Called: **THE PANTALOON CLIP**
THE BANDED CLIP

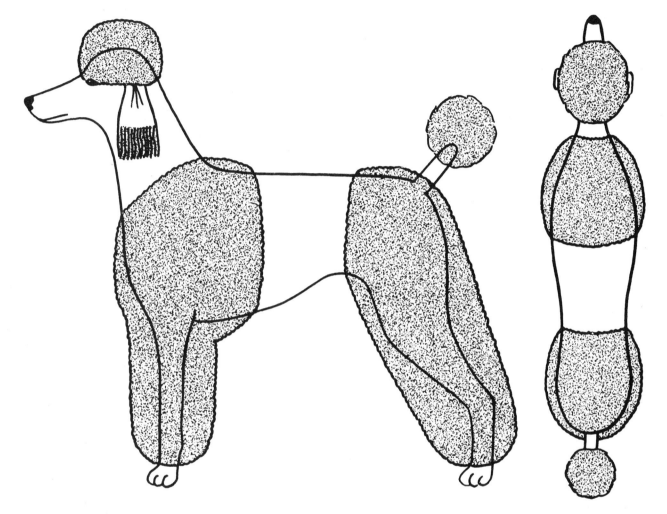

The New Yorker clip.

1. Follow instructions for clipping the feet.
2. Follow instructions for clipping the face. Clip the face clean or select any moustache style.
3. Follow instructions for clipping and scissoring the tail.
4. Follow instructions for clipping the stomach. Clip up to the middle of the dog, stopping at the last rib.
5. Sit the dog on the grooming table, facing you. Clip the back of the neck with a #15 blade. If you wish to use the topknot with the point in the center of the neck, scissor the point now **(A)**. Then use clippers to cut

119

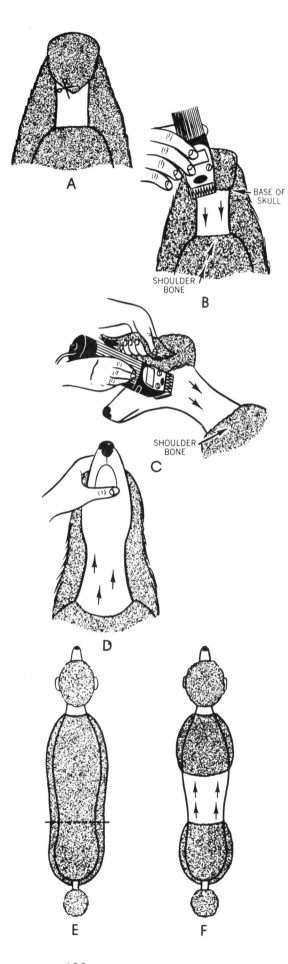

A

BASE OF SKULL

SHOULDER BONE

B

SHOULDER BONE

C

D

E F

around the point as instructed below. If you use a round topknot, hold the muzzle with your free hand, tilt the head down slightly and start the clippers at the base of the skull. Clip down to the shoulders (**B**). Do not clip below the shoulders or the dog's neck will appear too long. Clip the back of the neck working from ear to ear, using the clippers from the base of the skull down to the shoulders. Clip the sides of the neck by lifting each ear and clipping down from under the ear to the shoulder bone (**C**).

6. Use a # 10 blade to clip the front of the neck. Pointing the clippers upward, start about one inch below the Adam's apple on a Toy Poodle, two inches below on a Miniature and about three inches below in a Standard, and clip to the front of each ear. The front of the neck is rounded below the Adam's apple (**D**). When the neck is completely clipped, the line from front to back is rounded and looks like a necklace would around your own neck.

7. Stand the Poodle with his hindquarters facing you to start the pattern work. About one inch in front of the hipbones on Toy and Miniature Poodles and two inches in front of the hipbones on Standards, make a part across the Poodle's back (**E**). Be sure this part is in front of the hipbones and forward of the point where the back legs join the body on each side. If the part is made in back of the hipbones, the hindquarters will look weak. With a #10 blade, start at the part and clip up to the front of the dog, stopping about an inch or two before you reach the front legs (**F**). Keep clipping from the part line up to the front of the dog until you have clipped a wide band around the Poodle's middle. Clip the hair under the chest to complete the band (**G**). Be sure the clipped lines around the hips and ribs are straight. Make sure there are no straggly hairs on the dog's middle.

8. Stand the dog with his hindquarters facing you. Comb the hair on the back legs up and out to lift the hair and fluff the coat. The leg shape for the New Yorker Clip is the pantaloon style. If you are right handed, begin working on the leg at your right. If you are left handed, do the opposite. Scissor off any hairs that fall below the clipped line around the ankle (**H**). Then begin shaping the leg. The easiest way to scissor the pantaloon shape is to begin at the ankle and work up to the hip, stopping at the point where the leg joins the body. Scissor one part of the leg from the ankle up to the hip.

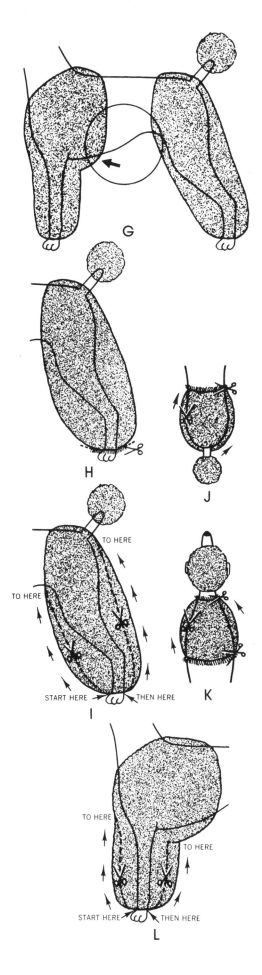

G

H

J

I

START HERE   THEN HERE

TO HERE

TO HERE

K

L

TO HERE

TO HERE

START HERE   THEN HERE

Then begin again at the ankle and scissor another part up to the hip. Work completely around the leg until you have the desired shape (**I**). Always follow the Poodle's natural conformation to show the angulation above the hock joint and the curve of the stifle joint. Always hold the scissors flat against the hair you are working on. Do not dig into the coat with the scissor points. If you are not satisfied with the leg shape, recomb the part you are working on and begin scissoring again. To scissor the hard-to-reach areas on the inside of the back leg, lift the opposite leg with your free hand. Scissor the opposite back leg. Be sure both legs are even in size and shape.

9. Comb the hair on the hips and hindquarters. Shape the hindquarters round with the scissors, following the natural contours of the dog's body. When scissoring the hair near the clipped line in front of the hip bones, comb it upward and forward. Then scissor off any hair that falls over the clipped line to make the pattern look neat (**J**).

10. Comb the hair on the ribs, shoulders and chest. Scissor any hair that falls over the clipped line at the ribs (**K**). Scissor the jacket to the same length as the hair on the hindquarters, following the natural contours of the body. Scissor the hair under the chest to the same length. Turn the dog to stand facing you and shape the front of the chest round, from shoulder to shoulder. Comb the hair up at the clipped line around the neck. Scissor any hair that extends over the clipped part of the neck to make the pattern look neat.

11. With the Poodle standing to face you, comb the hair on the front legs. Scissor off any hair that falls below the clipped line on the ankle. Then begin shaping the leg. Start at the ankle and scissor one part of the leg up to the elbow. Begin again at the ankle and scissor another part of the leg up to the elbow. Work completely around the leg (**L**), until you have the desired shape. If you are not satisfied with the leg shape, recomb the area you are working on and begin scissoring again. To scissor the hair on the hard-to-reach areas under the front leg, lift the leg under which you want to scissor and pull it gently forward to avoid cutting holds in the coat. Scissor the opposite front leg. Be sure both legs are even in size and shape.

12. Sit the Poodle on the grooming table, facing you. Comb the topknot hair upward and forward. Scissor a round or square-shaped topknot.

13. Select any ear style for the New Yorker Clip.

121

Variations of the New Yorker Clip

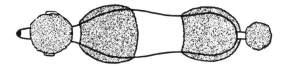

*Use the New Yorker body pattern for
all of these variations.*

THE BELL-BOTTOM NEW YORKER
(See Page 97)

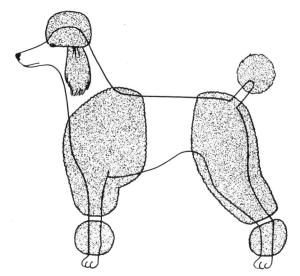

THE BOLERO NEW YORKER
(See Page 98)

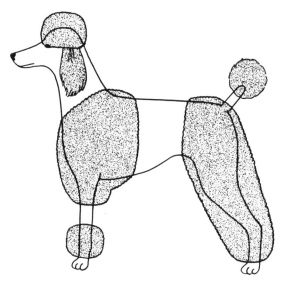

THE FIFTH AVENUE NEW YORKER
(See Page 99)

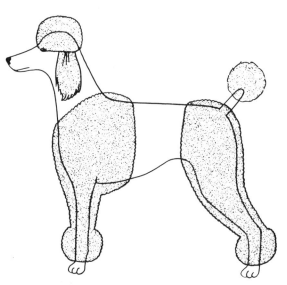

THE MIAMI NEW YORKER
(See Page 100)

122

The Dutch Clip

Also Called: MODERN DUTCH CLIP
ROYAL DUTCH CLIP
BOLERO CLIP

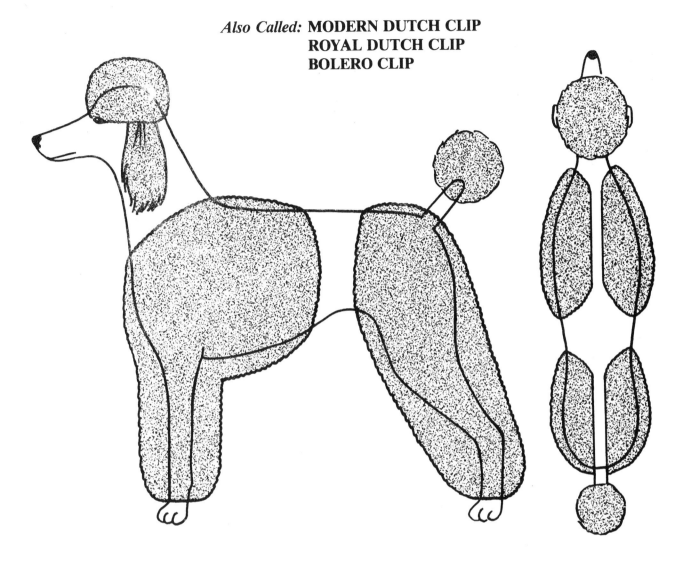

Dutch clip.

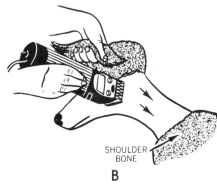

A

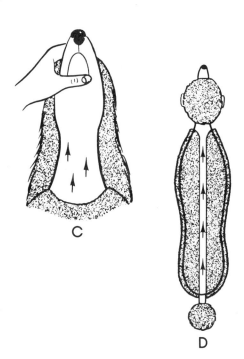

B

C

D

1. Follow instructions for clipping the feet.
2. Follow instructions for clipping the face. Clip the face clean or select any moustache style.
3. Follow instructions for clipping and scissoring the tail.
4. Follow instructions for clipping the stomach. Use a #10 blade. Clip up to the middle of the dog, stopping at the last rib.
5. Sit the Poodle on the grooming table, facing you. Clip the back of the neck with a #15 blade. Gently holding the dog's muzzle in your free hand, tilt the head down and start the clippers at the base of the skull. Clip down to the shoulders (**A**). Do not clip below the shoulders or the neck will look long and out of proportion. Clip the back of the neck by working from one ear to the other, using clippers from the base of the skull down to the shoulders. Clip the sides of the neck by lifting each ear and clipping down from under the ear to the shoulder bone (**B**).
6. Use a #10 blade to clip the front of the neck. Pointing clippers upward, start about one inch below the Adam's apple on a Toy Poodle, two inches below the Adam's apple on a Miniature and about three inches below on a Standard and clip to the front of each ear. The front part of the neck below the Adam's apple is rounded (**C**). When the neck is completely clipped, the line from front to back is rounded and looks like a necklace would around your own neck.
7. Stand the Poodle with his hindquarters facing you to begin pattern work. The first step in the Dutch Clip is to clip a strip from the base of the tail, up the center of the back to the neck. The width of this strip must be in proportion to the size of dog you are clipping for the Dutch pattern to look correct. The mistake most beginners make is clipping this strip too wide. Use a #⅝ blade on a Toy Poodle, a #⅞ or ⅝ on a Miniature, and a #10 or #15 on a Standard. Start the clippers at the base of the tail and clip straight up the center of the back to the neck (**D**). Be sure the dog stands still when you clip the strip. If he moves, it will be uneven and off-center. If you work on a fussy dog, have someone steady his front while you clip. If you are working on a small Poodle and do not own one of the narrow cutting

124

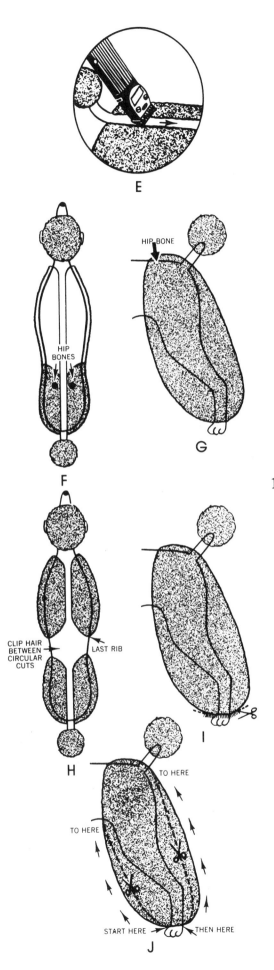

E

HIP BONE

HIP BONES

F

G

CLIP HAIR BETWEEN CIRCULAR CUTS

LAST RIB

H

I

TO HERE

TO HERE

START HERE   THEN HERE

J

blades, use a #10 blade to clip the strip. First use the scissors to cut, or chalk to mark the desired width of the strip. Then tilt the blade to the side (**E**), and use the edge to clip up one side of the body, then up the other side.

8. The next step in the Dutch Clip is to make a circular cut on each side of the hindquarters to shape the pantaloons on the back legs. Start at the center strip, about one to two inches in front of the hipbones. Use the clippers to make a circular cut on each side of the dog (**F**). make these circular cuts even. Always start these circular cuts in front of the hipbones to keep the clipped line on the loins *forward* of the point where the back legs meet the body (**G**). Clipping the circular cuts exactly at the point where the back legs meet the body makes the Poodle's hindquarters appear weak.

9. Begin at the center strip at the last rib. Clip a circular cut on each side of the dog (**H**). If you have clipped the stomach up to the last rib, as instructed in Step 4, the circular cut at the ribs now goes completely around the dog's middle and the jacket is formed. Clean off all hair on the dog's middle between the cuts around the back legs and the clipped lines around the ribs.
   Your pattern is now complete.

10. Comb the hair on the back legs up and out to fluff the coat. The shape of the leg for the Dutch Clip is the pantaloon style. If you are right handed, begin working on the leg at your right. If you are left handed, do the opposite. Scissor off any hairs that fall below the clipped line around the ankle (**I**). Then begin shaping the leg with scissors. The easiest way to scissor the pantaloon shape, is to begin at the ankle and work up to the hip, stopping at a point where the leg joins the body. Begin by scissoring one part of the leg from the ankle up to the hip. Then begin again at the ankle and scissor another part up to the hip. Use this method to work completely around the leg (**J**), until you have the desired shape. Always follow the dog's natural conformation and show the angulation above the hock joint and the curve of the stifle joint. Hold the scissors flat against the hair you work on, taking off a little hair at a time. Do not dig into the coat with the scissor points. If you are not satisfied with the leg shape, recomb the part you are working on, and begin again. To scissor the hard-to-reach areas on the inside of the back leg, lift the opposite leg with your free hand. Scissor the other back leg. Be sure both legs are even in size and shape.

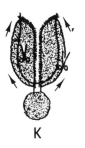   

K   L   M   N

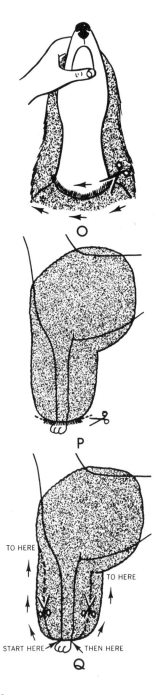

O

P

TO HERE

TO HERE

START HERE   THEN HERE

Q

11. Comb the hair on the hips and hindquarters. Continue scissoring up from the legs on each side, rounding the hindquarters (**K**). When scissoring near the center strip and around the circular cuts on the loins, comb the hair up and forward, then scissor around each pantaloon (**L**), to emphasize the pattern lines.

12. Comb the hair on the ribs, shoulders and chest up and out to fluff the coat. The hair on the jacket should be the same length as the hair on the hindquarters. Scissor the jacket round, following the natural contours of the body (**M**). When scissoring under the chest, make the hair the same length as on top. Comb the hair on each side of the center strip and around the cuts over the ribs. Scissor around these circular cuts and center strip (**N**), to emphasize the pattern lines. Turn the Poodle around to stand facing you. Scissor the front of the chest round, from shoulder to shoulder. Comb the hair up at the clipped line around the neck. Scissor around the clipped line (**O**), to make the pattern look neat.

13. With the Poodle standing facing you, comb the hair on the front legs. Use the comb in an up and out motion, to fluff the coat. Scissor any hair that falls below the clipped line around the ankle (**P**). Then begin shaping the leg. Start at the ankle and scissor part of the leg up to the elbow. Begin again at the ankle and scissor another part of the leg up to the elbow. Work completely around the leg (**Q**), until you have the desired shape. If you are not satisfied with the leg shape, recomb the hair and begin scissoring again. To scissor the hard-to-reach areas under the front leg, lift the leg under which you want to scissor and pull it forward to avoid cutting holes in the coat. Scissor the other front leg. Be sure both legs are even in size and shape.

14. Comb the topknot hair upward and forward. Scissor a round or square topknot.

15. Select any ear style for the Dutch Clip.

Variations of the Dutch Clip

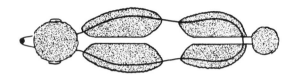

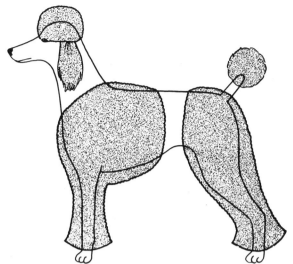

Use the Dutch body pattern for all of these variations.

THE BELL-BOTTOM DUTCH
(See Page 97)

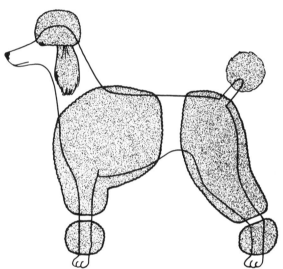

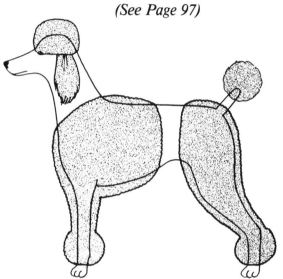

THE BOLERO DUTCH
(See Page 98)

THE MIAMI DUTCH
(See Page 100)

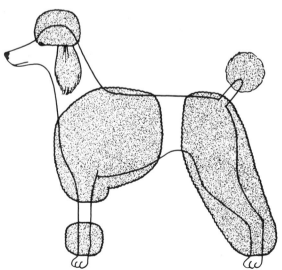

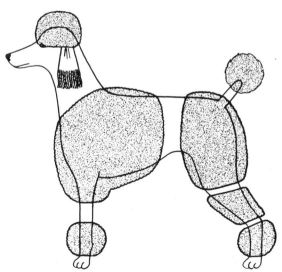

THE FIFTH AVENUE DUTCH
(See Page 99)

THE SADDLE DUTCH
(See Page 101)

The Pittsburgh Dutch

Also Called: **THE MODIFIED DUTCH**
THE SPLIT-T

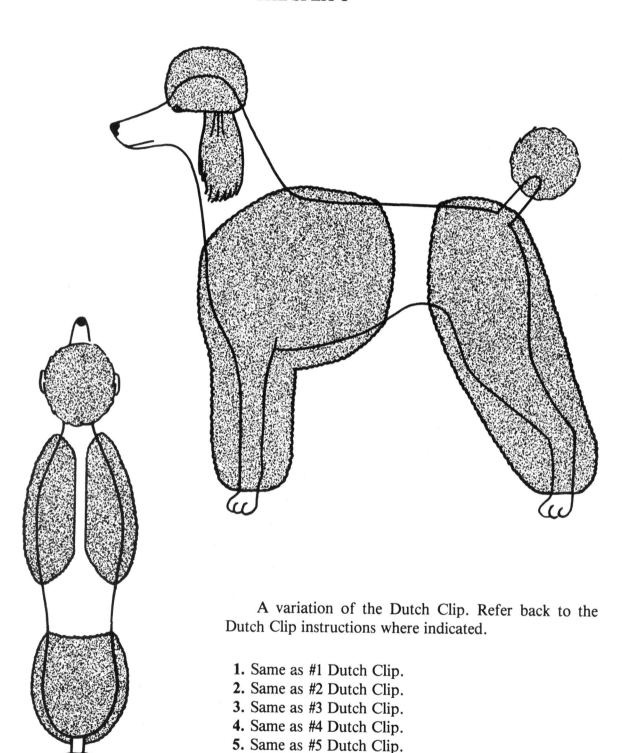

A variation of the Dutch Clip. Refer back to the Dutch Clip instructions where indicated.

1. Same as #1 Dutch Clip.
2. Same as #2 Dutch Clip.
3. Same as #3 Dutch Clip.
4. Same as #4 Dutch Clip.
5. Same as #5 Dutch Clip.
6. Same as #6 Dutch Clip.
7. Stand the Poodle with his hindquarters facing you to begin pattern work. Use a comb to part the hair over

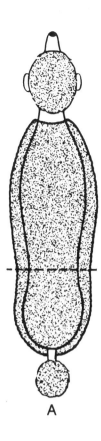

A

the hindquarters in front of the hipbones (**A**). Make this part one inch in front of the hipbones on a Toy Poodle and two inches in front of the hipbones on a Miniature or Standard Poodle.

8. The first step in the Pittsburgh Dutch pattern is to clip a strip from this "part" line up the center of the back to the neck. Use a #⅝ blade on a Toy, a #⅞ or #⅝ on a Miniature and a #10 on a Standard. Start at the part line and clip a strip up the center of the back to the neck (**B**).

9. Clip off all hair on each side of the loin from the part line up to the last rib (**C**). Use corner of the clipper blade to round the edges of the strip at the last rib.

10. Same as #10 Dutch Clip.

11. Comb hair on hips and hindquarters. Continue scissoring up from the legs on each side, shaping the hindquarters round. When scissoring near the clipped line in front of the hipbones, comb the hair up and forward, then cut off any hair that falls over the line to emphasize the pattern.

12. Same as #12 Dutch Clip.

13. Same as #13 Dutch Clip.

14. Same as #14 Dutch Clip.

15. Same as #15 Dutch Clip.

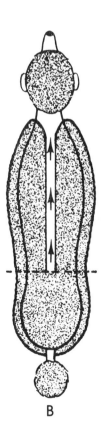

B

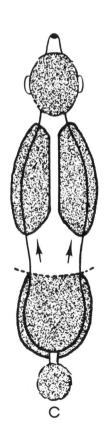

C

The Chicago Dutch

Also Called: **THE T-CLIP**
THE TUXEDO
THE MODIFIED DUTCH
THE SCOTTSDALE DUTCH

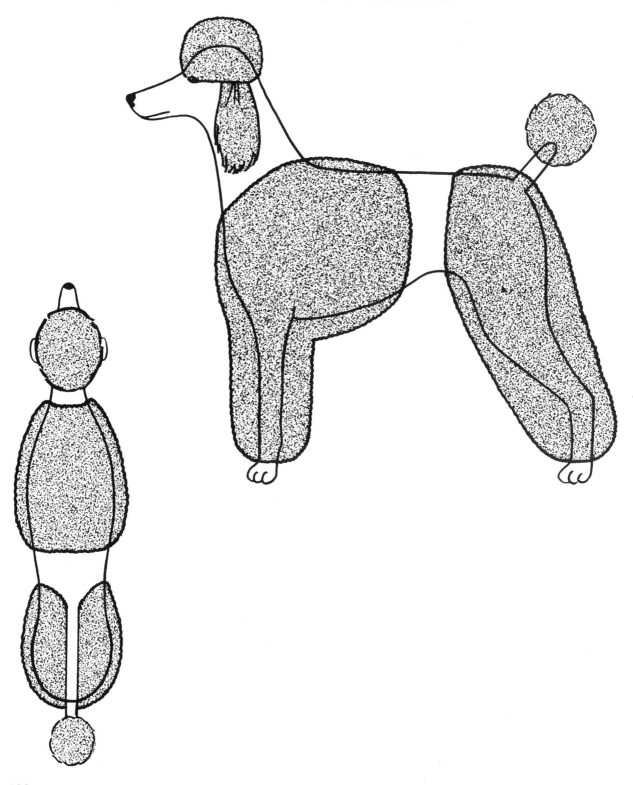

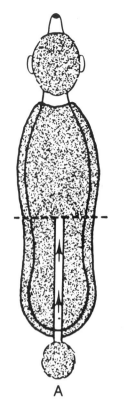

A

A variation of the Dutch Clip. Refer back to the Dutch Clip instructions where indicated.

1. Same as #1 Dutch Clip.
2. Same as #2 Dutch Clip.
3. Same as #3 Dutch Clip.
4. Same as #4 Dutch Clip.
5. Same as #5 Dutch Clip.
6. Same as #6 Dutch Clip.
7. Stand the Poodle with his hindquarters facing you to begin pattern work. Use a comb to make a part completely around the dog's middle at the last rib. Be sure the part is even. The first step in the Chicago Dutch pattern is to clip a strip from the base of the tail up the center of the back to the last rib. Use a #⅝ blade on a Toy Poodle, a #⅞ or #⅝ on a Miniature Poodle and a #10 on a Standard. Start at the base of the tail and clip a strip up the center of the back between the hipbones to the "part" line at the last rib (**A**).
8. The next step in the Chicago Dutch Clip is to make a circular cut on each side of the hindquarters to shape the pantaloons on the back legs. Start at the center strip, about one to two inches above the hipbones, and make a circular cut on each side of the dog (**B**).
9. Clip the hair on the dog's middle between the circular cuts around the back legs and the "part" around the last rib (**C**).
10. Same as #10 Dutch Clip.
11. Same as #11 Dutch Clip.
12. Comb the hair on the ribs, shoulders, and chest up and out to fluff the coat. Scissor the jacket round, following the natural contour of the dog's body. Scissor the hair under the chest the same length as on top. Turn the Poodle to stand facing you. Scissor the front of the chest round, from shoulder to shoulder. Comb the hair up at the clipped line around the neck. Scissor around the clipped line to make the pattern look neat.
13. Same as #13 Dutch Clip.
14. Same as #14 Dutch Clip.
15. Same as #15 Dutch Clip.

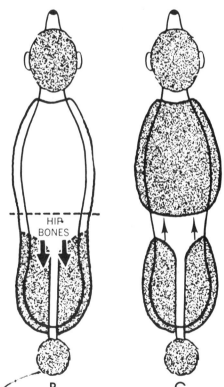

B   C

Because this is a different body pattern, you may use the Miami, Bell-Bottom, Bolero, Fifth Avenue or Saddle leg styles with this clip for 5 new variations.

The Criss-Cross Dutch

Also Called: **THE BANDED DUTCH**

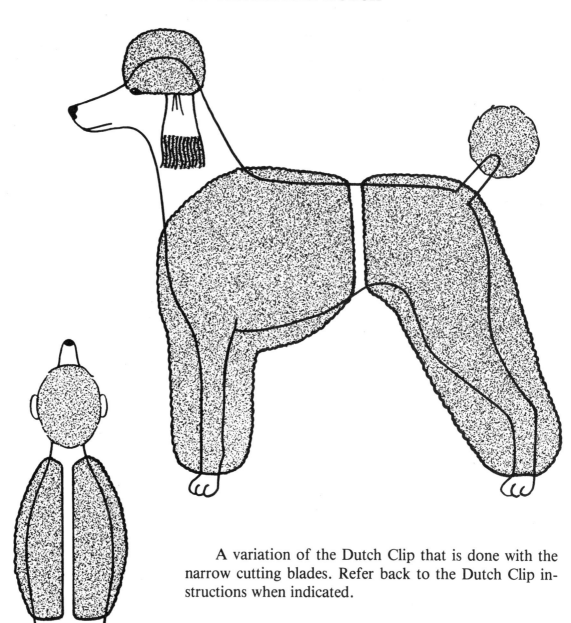

A variation of the Dutch Clip that is done with the narrow cutting blades. Refer back to the Dutch Clip instructions when indicated.

1. Same as #1 Dutch Clip.
2. Same as #2 Dutch Clip.
3. Same as #3 Dutch Clip.
4. Same as #4 Dutch Clip.
5. Same as #5 Dutch Clip.
6. Same as #6 Dutch Clip.
7. Stand the Poodle with his hindquarters facing you to begin pattern work. The first step in the Criss-Cross Dutch pattern is to make a narrow strip from the base of the tail up the center of the back to the neck. Use a #⅝ blade on a Toy Poodle, a #⅞ on a Miniature and a

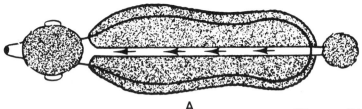

A

#⅝ on a Standard. Start the clippers at the base of the tail and clip a strip straight up the center of the back (**A**). Be sure the dog stands still while you clip this strip. If he is fussy, have someone steady his front so the strip is not off-center.

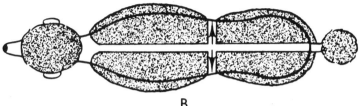

B

8. The next step in the Criss-Cross Dutch pattern is to make a circular strip around the middle of the dog. Using the same narrow cutting blade, start at the last rib and clip a strip around each side of the dog (**B**).
9. Use the corner of the clipper blade to round the edges of the strips at the neck and center of the back (**C**).
10. Same as #10 Dutch Clip.

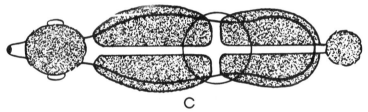

C

11. Comb the hair on the hips and hindquarters. Shape the hindquarters round, following the natural contours of the body. When scissoring near the narrow center strip, comb the hair up and forward, then scissor off all hair that falls over the clipped lines to make the pattern look neat.
12. Comb the hair on the ribs, shoulders and chest up and out. Scissor the jacket to a round shape following the natural contours of the body. Scissor the hair under the chest to the same length as on top. Comb the hair near the center strip around the last rib, then scissor off any hairs that fall over the clipped lines to make the pattern look neat.
13. Same as #13 Dutch Clip.
14. Same as #14 Dutch Clip.
15. Same as #15 Dutch Clip.

Because this is a different body pattern, you may use the Miami, Bell-Bottom, Bolero, Fifth Avenue, Saddle and Continental leg styles with this clip for six new variations.

The Royal Dutch

Also Called: **THE HOLLAND DUTCH**
THE PALM SPRINGS
THE COWBOY
THE MODERN

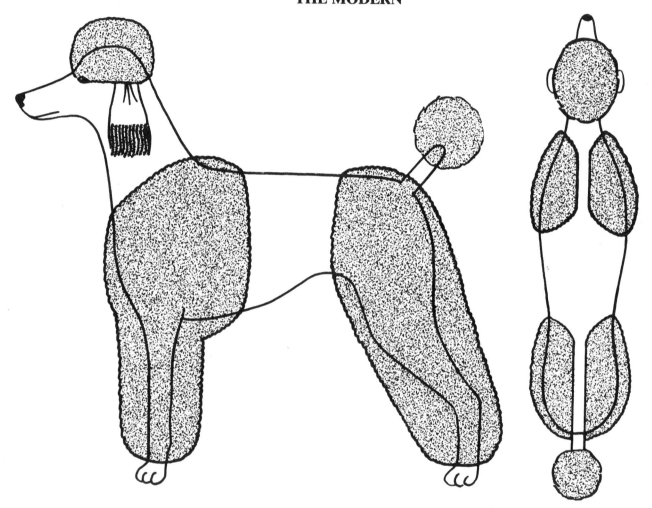

A variation of the Dutch Clip which differs only in the clipping of the jacket. The Dutch jacket line is clipped at the last rib and the Royal Dutch jacket line is clipped just behind the front legs.

Follow Dutch Clip instructions for clipping feet, face, tail, neck and stomach. Stand the dog on the grooming table with his hindquarters facing you. Follow Dutch Clip instructions for clipping center strip and circular cuts over back legs. Then start at the center strip about one to two inches behind the front legs. Clip the circular cut on each side of the ribs to form the jacket. Clean off all hair on the dog's middle between the back pantaloons and the jacket. Scissor the legs and body hair as instructed in the Dutch Clip. Select any topknot or ear style for the Royal Dutch.

Since this is a different body pattern, you may use the Miami, Bell-Bottom, Bolero, Fifth Avenue or Saddle leg styles for five additional variations of this clip.

134

The Pajama Dutch

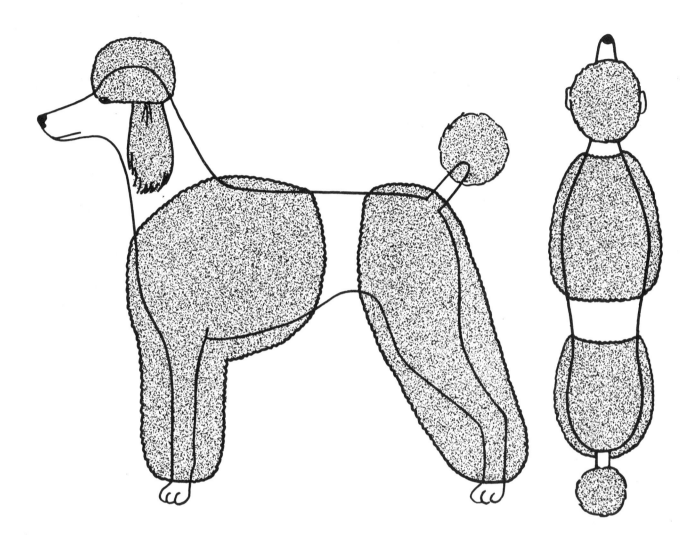

Follow Dutch Clip instructions for clipping feet, face, tail, neck and stomach. Stand the Poodle with his hindquarters facing you to begin pattern work. About one inch in front of the hipbones on Toy Poodles and two inches in front of the hipbones on Miniatures and Standards, make a circular part across the back. Be sure the part is even. Use a #10 blade and clip from the "part" line up to the last rib. Keep clipping from the part line up to the last rib until you have made a clipped band completely around the middle of the Poodle. Scissor the back legs and hindquarters as instructed in the Dutch Clip. Scissor off any hair that falls over the clipped lines around the hips and last rib to make the pattern look neat. Comb the jacket hair. Scissor the jacket, chest and front legs as instructed in the Dutch Clip. Select any topknot or ear style for the Pajama Dutch pattern.

Since this is a different body pattern, you may use the Miami, Bell-Bottom, Bolero, Fifth Avenue or Saddle leg styles for five additional variations.

The Continental Dutch

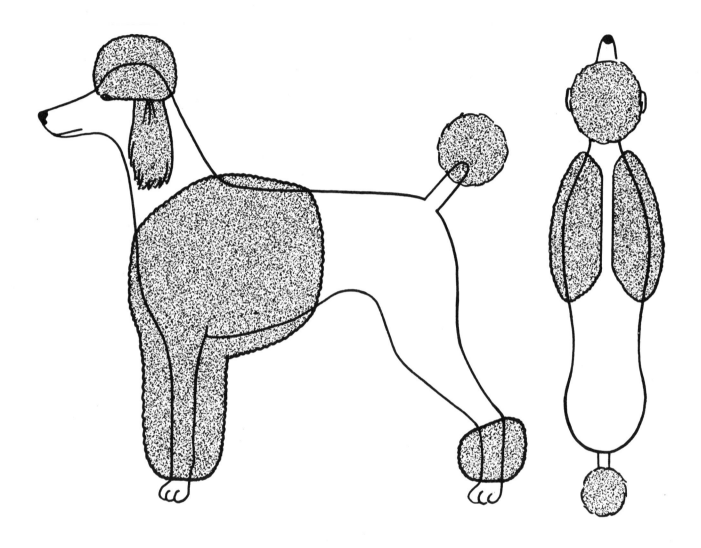

Follow Dutch Clip instructions for clipping feet, face, tail and neck. Stand the dog with his hindquarters facing you. Use a #10 blade. Pointing clippers upward, start at the hock joint and clip the hair from the outside and inside of each back leg. Continue clipping up over the hips and stomach and remove all hair on the hindquarters up to the last rib. Be sure the clipped line is even around the last rib. Clip the center strip and front part of the Dutch jacket as instructed in the Dutch Clip. Scissor the hair below the hock joint on each back leg into a bracelet. Comb the body hair. Scissor any hair that falls over the clipped jacket line at the last rib and center strip to emphasize the pattern. Then scissor the jacket, chest and front legs as instructed in the Dutch Clip. Select any topknot or ear style for this clip.

136

The Sweetheart Clip

Also Called: **THE HEART**

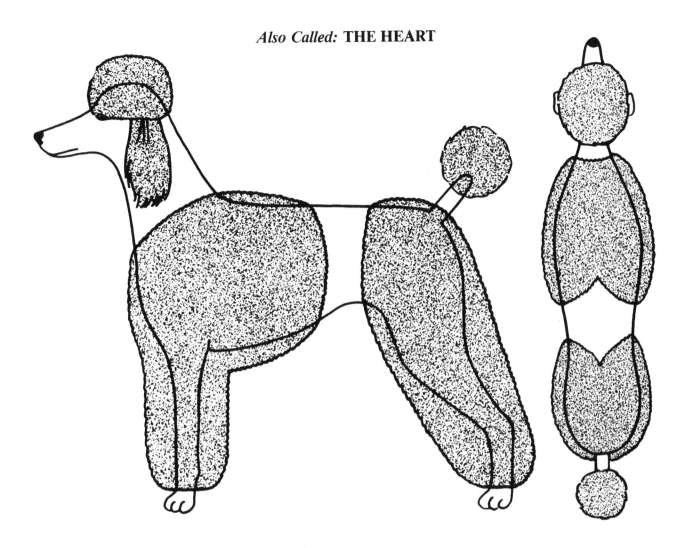

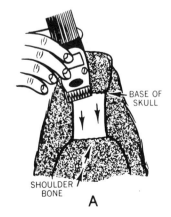

A

SHOULDER BONE

BASE OF SKULL

1. Follow instructions for clipping the feet.
2. Follow instructions for clipping the face. Clip the face clean or select any moustache style.
3. Follow instructions for clipping and scissoring the tail.
4. Follow instructions for clipping the stomach. Clip up to the middle of the dog, stopping at the last rib.
5. Sit the Poodle on the grooming table, facing you. Clip the back of the neck with a #15 blade. Gently holding the dog's muzzle with your free hand, tilt the head down and start clippers at the base of the skull. Clip down to the shoulders (**A**). Do not clip below the shoulders or the dog's neck will look long and out of proportion. Clip the back of the neck working from one ear to the other, using the clippers from the base of the skull down to the shoulders. Clip the sides of the neck by lifting each ear and clipping down from under the ear to the shoulder bone (**B**).

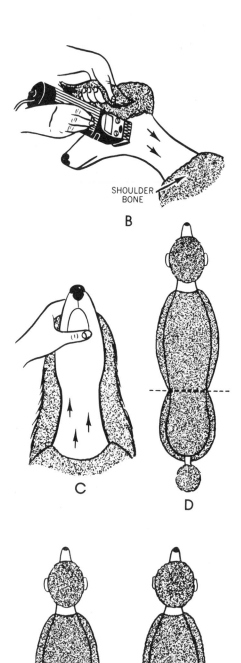

SHOULDER BONE

B

C

D

E   F

6. Use a #10 blade to clip the front of the neck. Pointing clippers upward, start about one inch below the Adam's apple on a Toy Poodle, two inches below the Adam's apple on a Miniature and about three inches below on a Standard, and clip to the front of each ear. The front of the neck below the Adam's apple is rounded (**C**). When the neck is completely clipped, the line from front to back looks like a necklace would around your own neck.

7. Stand the dog on the grooming table with the hindquarters facing you. Study the illustration of the Sweetheart pattern and notice that two hearts are clipped on the back. Begin pattern work by making a part over the hindquarters in front of the hipbones (**D**). If you are working on a Toy Poodle, make the part one inch in front of the hipbones. On a Miniature, make the part two inches in front of the hipbones. On a Standard, make the part three inches in front of the hipbones. To shape the hearts properly, this part must always be made in front of the hipbones and forward of the spot where the back legs join the body.

Use a #10 blade. Start from the part line and clip up to the last rib. Make a band around the dog's middle by clipping from the part up to the last rib (**E**).

8. Now you are ready to clip the hearts. The point of each heart must be in the center of the back. The pattern will be uneven if they are off-center. To avoid making a mistake with the clippers, cut the heart shapes with the scissors before you clip. Then use the edge of the clipper blade to clip the heart points (**F**).

9. Stand the Poodle with his hindquarters facing you. Comb the hair on the back legs up and out to fluff the coat. The shape of the Sweetheart leg is the familiar pantaloon style. First, scissor off any hairs that fall below the clipped line around the ankle (**G**). Then begin shaping the leg. The easiest way to scissor the pantaloon shape is to begin at the ankle and work up to the hip, stopping at the point where the leg joins the body. Scissor one part of the leg from the ankle up to the hip, then begin again at the ankle and scissor another part up to the hip. Work completely around the leg (**H**), until you have the desired shape. Remember to follow the dog's natural angulation above the hock joint and at the curve of the stifle joints. Always hold the scissors flat against the hair you are working on. Do not dig into the coat with the scissor points. If you are not satisfied with the leg shape, recomb the part you are working on and begin scissoring again. To scissor the hard-to-reach areas on

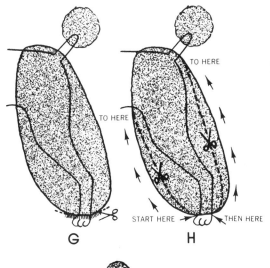

G

H

TO HERE

TO HERE

START HERE → ← THEN HERE

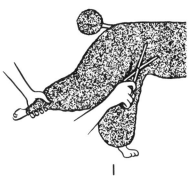

I

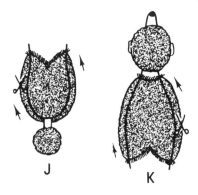

J

K

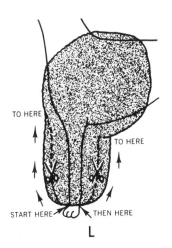

TO HERE

TO HERE

START HERE → ← THEN HERE

L

the inside of the back leg, lift the opposite leg with your free hand. Scissor the other back leg. Be sure both legs are even in size and shape.

10. Comb the hair on the hips and hindquarters. Shape the hindquarters round, following the natural contours of the dog's body. If you have difficulty scissoring the hair on the loin, lift the back leg with your free hand and pull it gently back (**I**), to avoid cutting holes in the coat. When scissoring near the clipped heart on the hips, comb the hair up and forward. Scissor any hair that falls over the clipped lines (**J**), to make the pattern look neat.

11. Comb the hair on the ribs, shoulders and chest. Scissor any hair that falls over the clipped heart at the last rib (**K**), to make the pattern look neat. Scissor the jacket to the same length as the hair on the hindquarters, following the natural contours of the body. Hold the scissors flat against the hair you work on and take a little hair off at a time. The easiest way to shape the jacket is to start at the last rib and scissor a section up to the neck. Then begin again at the last rib and scissor another part up to the neck. Keep working from the ribs up to the neck until the jacket is shaped. Turn the Poodle to face you and scissor the front of the chest round from shoulder to shoulder. Comb the hair up near the clipped part of the neck. Scissor any hairs that extend over the clipped line to make the pattern look neat.

12. Stand the Poodle to face you. Comb the hair on the front legs up and out to fluff the coat. Scissor any hairs that fall below the clipped line around the ankle. Then begin shaping the leg. Start at the ankle and scissor a part of the leg up to the elbow. Begin again at the ankle and scissor another part of the leg up to the elbow. Work completely around the leg (**L**), until you have the desired shape. If you are not satisfied with the leg shape, recomb the part you are working on and begin scissoring again. To scissor the hard-to-reach areas under the front leg, lift the leg under which you want to scissor and pull it gently forward, to avoid cutting holes in the coat. Scissor the opposite front leg. Be sure to make both front legs even in size and shape.

13. Select any topknot shape for the Sweetheart Clip.

14. Select any ear style.

Variations of the Sweetheart Clip

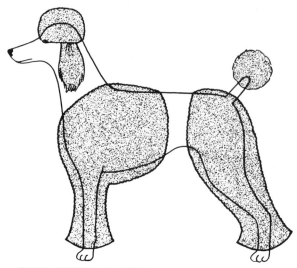

THE BELL-BOTTOM SWEETHEART
(See Page 97)

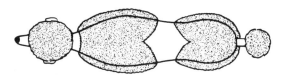

Use the Sweetheart Body Clip for all of these variations.

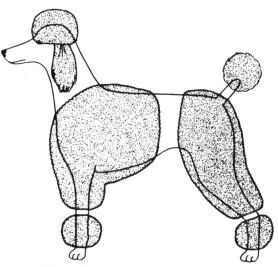

THE BOLERO SWEETHEART
(See Page 98)

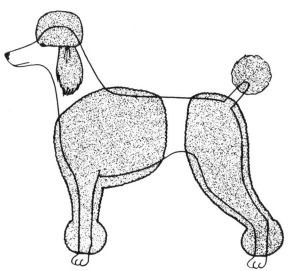

THE FIFTH AVENUE SWEETHEART
(See Page 100)

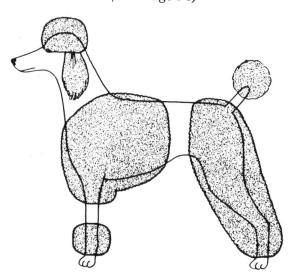

THE MIAMI SWEETHEART
(See Page 99)

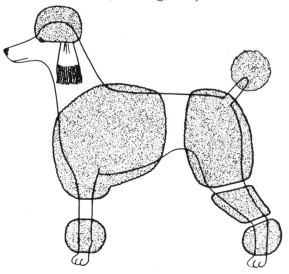

THE SADDLE SWEETHEART
(See Page 101)

THE CONTINENTAL SWEETHEART

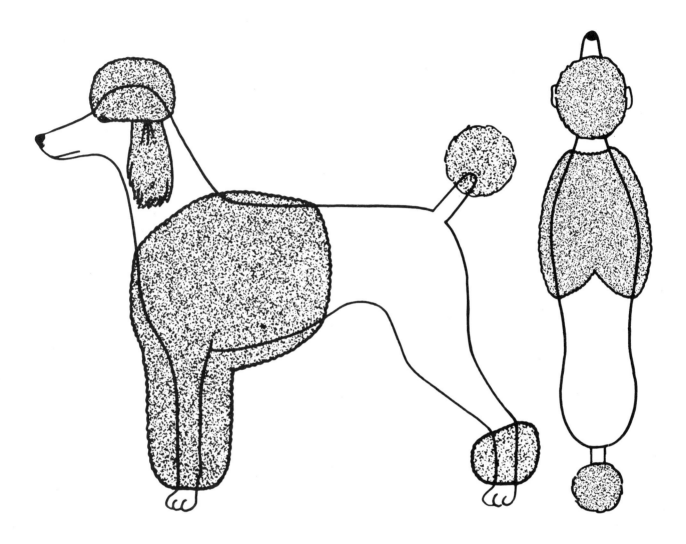

Follow Sweetheart Clip instructions for clipping feet, face, tail and neck. Stand the dog with the hindquarters facing you. Use a #10 blade. Pointing clippers upward, start at the hock joint and clip the hair from the outside and inside of each back leg. Continue clipping up over the hips and stomach and remove all hair on the hindquarters up to the last rib. Be sure the clipped line is even around the last rib. Clip the front part of the heart pattern starting at the last rib, as instructed in the Sweetheart Clip. Scissor the hair below the hock joint on each back leg into a bracelet. Comb the body hair. Scissor the jacket, chest and front legs as instructed in the Sweetheart Clip. Select any topknot and ear style for this clip.

The Bandero Clip

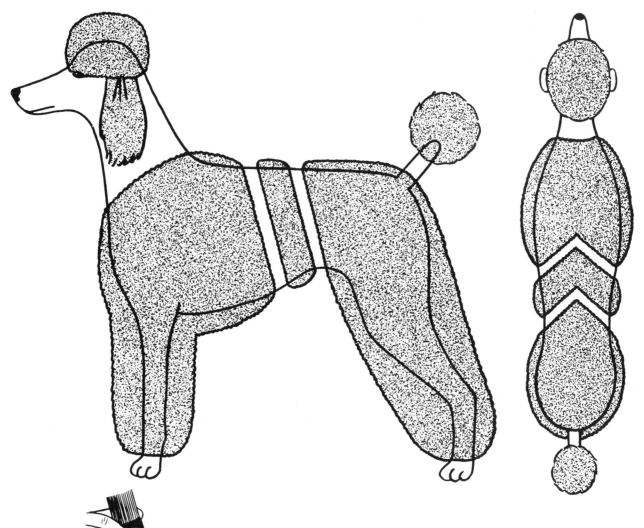

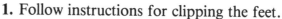

1. Follow instructions for clipping the feet.
2. Follow instructions for clipping the face. Clip the face clean or select any moustache style.
3. Follow instructions for clipping and scissoring the tail.
4. Follow instructions for clipping the stomach. Use a #10 blade. Clip up to the middle of the dog, stopping at the last rib.
5. Sit the Poodle on the grooming table, facing you. Clip the back of the neck with a #15 blade. Gently hold the dog's muzzle with your free hand, tilt the head down and start the clippers at the base of the skull. Clip down to the shoulders (**A**). Do not clip below the shoulders or the dog's neck will look long and out of proportion. Clip the back of the neck, working from one ear to the other, using the clippers from the base of the skull down to the shoulders. Clip the sides of the neck by lifting each ear and clipping down from under the ear to the shoulder bone (**B**).

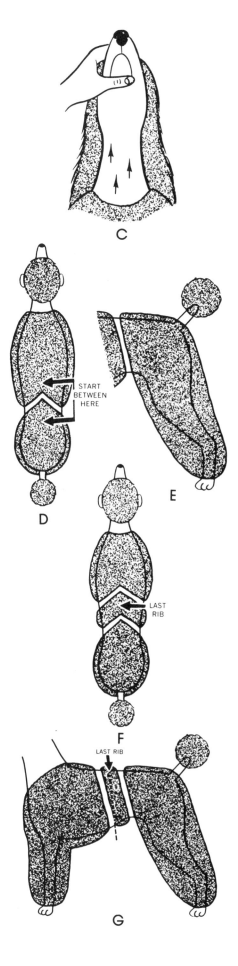

C

START
BETWEEN
HERE

D

E

LAST
RIB

F

LAST RIB

G

6. Use a #10 blade to clip the front of the neck. Pointing clippers upward, start about one inch below the Adam's apple on a Toy Poodle, about two inches below on a Miniature and about three inches below on a Standard and clip to the front of each ear. The front part of the neck below the Adam's apple is rounded (**C**). When the neck is completely clipped from front to back, the line is rounded and looks like a necklace would around your own neck.

7. Stand the Poodle on the grooming table with the hind-quarters facing you. Study the top and side views of the Bandero illustration and notice that there are two chevron-shaped bands clipped on the dog's back. These clipped bands must be in proportion to the size dog you are clipping. Use a $\#^5/_8$ blade to clip the bands on a Toy Poodle, a $\#^7/_8$ or $\#^8/_8$ blade for a Miniature Poodle, and a #10 or #15 blade for a Standard Poodle. The Bandero Clip is easy to do, but the clipped bands must be at the proper location on the body. Begin pattern work by clipping the lower band. Start at a point in the center of the back, half-way between the hip-bones and last rib (**D**), and clip a chevron-shaped band. The point of the chevron must be in the center of the back. To avoid making a mistake with the clippers, cut the shape of the point with scissors before you start clipping. In a side view of this lower band (**E**), notice that the bottoms of the band end just about where the back legs join the body.

8. Clip the upper band. Begin again in the center of the back in front of the last rib (**F**). Clip another chevron-shaped band, even in size and shape with the lower band. In a side view of this upper band shown (**G**), notice that the bottoms of the band end at the last rib. If you follow these instructions, the clipped bands will always be correct in size, shape and position, whatever the size of Poodle you clip.

9. Stand the Poodle with the hindquarters facing you. Comb the hair on the back legs up and out. The leg should be scissored in the familiar "pantaloon" style. If you are right handed, begin working on the leg at your right. If you are left handed, do the opposite. Scissor off any hairs that fall below the clipped line around the ankle (**H**). Then begin shaping the leg. The easiest way to scissor the pantaloon shape is to begin at the ankle and work up to the hip, stopping at the point where the leg joins the body. Scissor one part of the leg from the ankle up to the hip, then begin again at the ankle and scissor another part up to the hip. Work

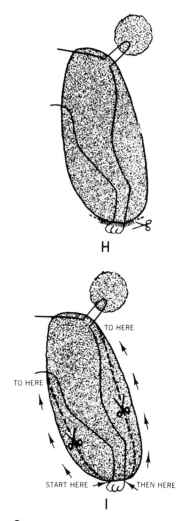

H

I

TO HERE

TO HERE

START HERE — THEN HERE

completely around the leg (**I**), until you have the desired shape. Always follow the dog's natural conformation and show the angulation above the hock joint and at the curve of the stifle joint. Hold the scissors flat against the hair you work on, taking a little hair off at a time. Do not dig into the coat with the scissor points. If you are not satisfied with the leg shape, recomb the part you are working on and begin scissoring again. To scissor the hard-to-reach areas on the inside of the back leg, lift the opposite leg with your free hand. Scissor the other back leg. Be sure both legs are even in size and shape.

10. Comb the hair on the hips, hindquarters, back, ribs and shoulders to fluff out the coat. Scissor this hair to an even length, following the natural contours of the dog's body. Hold the scissors flat against the hair you are working on to take a little hair off at a time. When scissoring near the clipped bands, comb the hair up and forward. Then scissor off any straggly hairs that fall over the clipped lines (**J**), to make the pattern look neat. Scissor the hair under the chest to the same length as on the top and sides of the body. Turn the Poodle around to stand facing you. Scissor the front of the chest round, from shoulder to shoulder. Comb the hair near the clipped part of the neck. Scissor any hairs that extend over the clipped line, to make the pattern look neat.

11. Comb the hair on the front legs. Use the comb in an up and out motion to fluff the coat. Scissor any hair that falls below the clipped line around the ankle. Then begin shaping the leg. Start at the ankle and scissor part of the leg up to the elbow. Begin again at the ankle and scissor another part of the leg up to the elbow. Work completely around the leg (**K**), until you have the desired shape. If you are not satisfied with the leg shape, recomb the part you are working on and begin scissoring again. To scissor the hard-to-reach areas under the front leg, lift the leg and pull it gently forward to avoid cutting holes in the coat. Scissor the other front leg even in size and shape.

12. Select any topknot style.

13. Select any ear style.

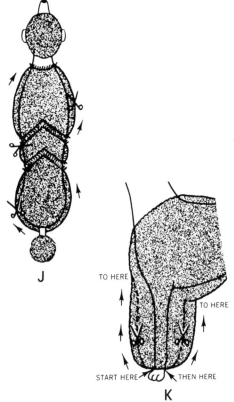

J

K

TO HERE

TO HERE

START HERE — THEN HERE

144

Variations of the Bandero Clip

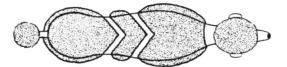

*Use the Bandero Body Pattern for
all of these variations.*

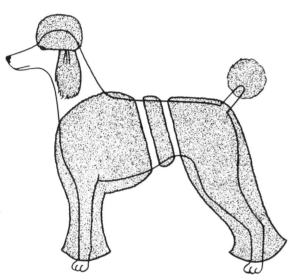

THE BELL-BOTTOM BANDERO
(See Page 97)

THE BOLERO BANDERO
(See Page 98)

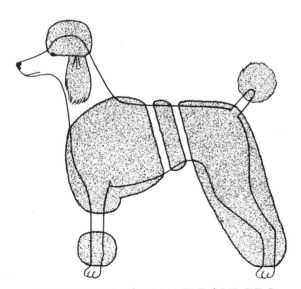

THE FIFTH AVENUE BANDERO
(See Page 99)

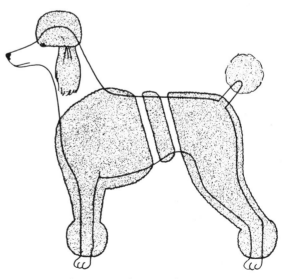

THE MIAMI BANDERO
(See Page 100)

The Rio Bandero

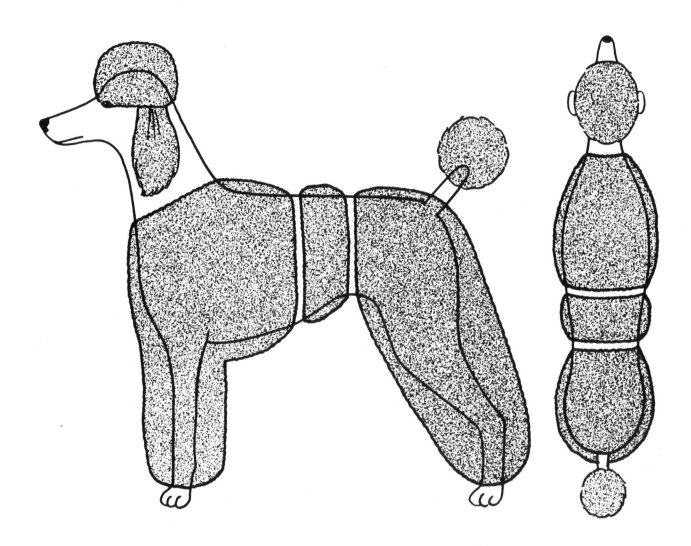

A variation of the Bandero Clip. Refer back to the Bandero instructions where indicated.

1. Same as #1 of Bandero Clip.
2. Same as #2 of Bandero Clip.
3. Same as #3 of Bandero Clip.
4. Clip stomach with #10 blade. Pointing clippers upward, start above the testicles or vulva and clip to the point where the back leg joins the body. Do not clip up to the last rib as you would do for other pet clips.
5. Same as #6 of Bandero Clip.
7. Stand the Poodle on the grooming table with his hindquarters facing you. Study the top and side views of the

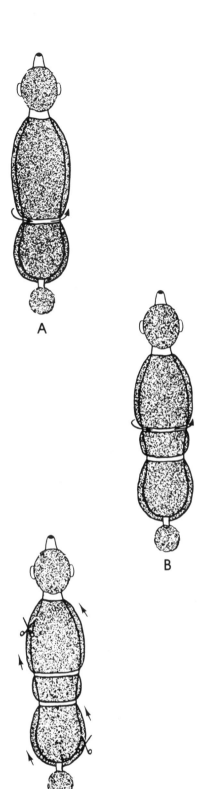

A

B

C

Rio Bandero clip. Notice that there are two circular bands clipped around the dog's body. These clipped bands must be in proportion to the size of dog you are clipping. Use a #⅝ blade to clip the bands on a Toy Poodle, a #⅞ or #⅞ on a Miniature and a #10 or #15 on a Standard. Begin pattern work by clipping the lower circular band. Start about one inch in front of the hipbones on a Toy, one and one-half inches on a Miniature and two inches on a Standard, and clip a circular band around the body (**A**). Clip the stomach up to this band line to make the line circle the body.

8. Clip the upper circular band. Begin about one inch in front of the last rib on a Toy Poodle, one and one-half inches on a Miniature and two inches on a Standard, and clip another circular band (**B**), even in size and shape with the lower band. Since this upper band completely encircles the body, remember to clip under the chest. If you follow these instructions, the bands will always be correct in size, shape and position, whatever size of Poodle you clip.

9. Same as #9 of Bandero Clip.

10. Comb the hair on the hips, hindquarters, back, ribs and shoulders to fluff out the coat. Scissor this hair to an even length, following the natural shape of the dog's body (**C**). When scissoring near the clipped bands, comb the hair up and forward. Then scissor off any straggly hairs that fall over the clipped lines to make the pattern look neat. Turn the Poodle around to stand facing you. Scissor the front of the chest round, from shoulder to shoulder. Comb the hair near the clipped line around the neck. Scissor any hairs that extend over the clipped part to make the pattern look neat.

11. Same as #11 of Bandero Clip.

12. Same as #12 of Bandero Clip.

13. Same as #13 of Bandero Clip.

Since this is a different body pattern, you may use the Bolero, Bell-Bottom, Fifth Avenue, Miami and Saddle leg styles for five new variations.

The Diamond Clip

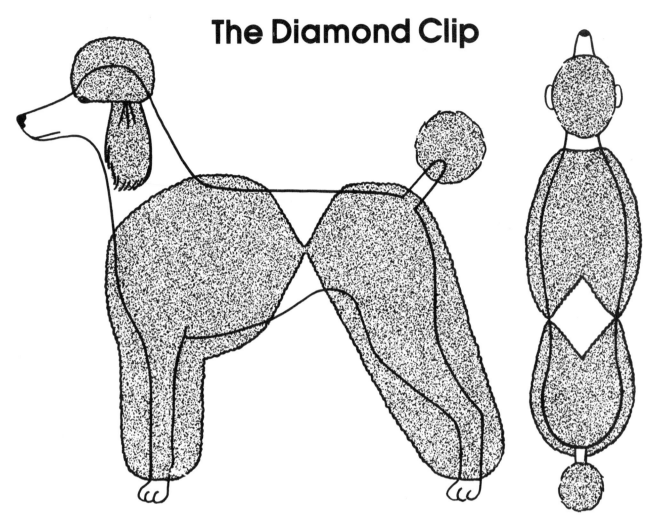

1. Follow instructions for clipping the feet.
2. Follow instructions for clipping the face. Clip the face clean or select any moustache style.
3. Follow instructions for clipping the stomach. Clip up to the last rib with a #10 blade.
4. Sit the Poodle on the grooming table, facing you. Clip the back of the neck with a #15 blade. Hold the dog's muzzle with your free hand, tilt the head down and clip from the base of the skull to the shoulders (**A**). Clip the

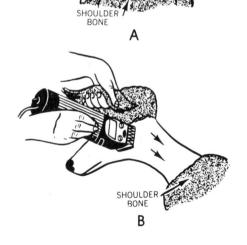

A

BASE OF SKULL

SHOULDER BONE

B

SHOULDER BONE

C

D

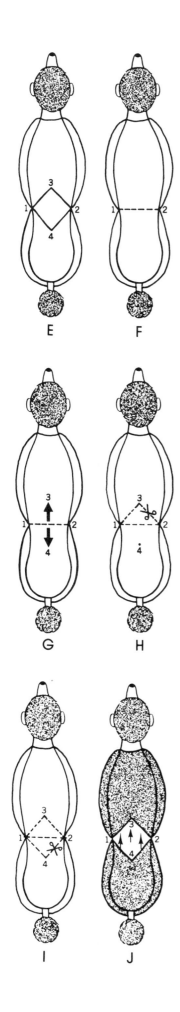

E   F

G   H

I   J

back of the neck, working from one ear to the other, using the clippers from the base of the skull down to the shoulders. Clip the sides of the neck by lifting each ear and clipping down from under the ear to the shoulder bone (**B**). You might consider using the V-shaped topknot with the Diamond Clip. As explained in the Topknot Chapter, the V-shaped topknot has a point centered on the back of the neck. This point extends one-half inch below the base of the skull on Toy Poodles, three-quarters to one inch below the base of the skull on Miniatures and about two inches below on Standards. Scissor the shape of the point to be sure it is properly centered. Then tilt the head down and clip around the V-shape (**C**).

5. Use a #10 blade to clip the front of the neck. Pointing clippers upward, start about one inch below the Adam's apple on a Toy Poodle, two inches below on a Miniature and about three inches below on a Standard, and clip to the front of each ear. The front part of the neck below the Adam's apple is rounded (**D**).

6. Stand the Poodle on the grooming table with his hindquarters facing you. Study **Sketch E** of the Diamond pattern. Points 1 and 2 must be at the last rib, half-way between the top and underside of the dog. Points 3 and 4 must be in the center of the back. Begin pattern work. Use a comb to make a part completely around the last rib (**F**). Be sure the part is even, for Points 1 and 2 will be at this line.

Use chalk to mark Point 3. Mark a dot in the center of the back, in front of the part line (**G**). Make this dot one to one and one-half inches in front of the part on Toys, two inches in front of the part on Miniatures, and three to four inches in front of the part on Standards. Use chalk to mark Point **4**. Make another dot in the center of the back (**G**), in back of the part line. Make this dot one to one and one-half inches in back of the part on Toys, two inches on Miniatures, and three to four inches on Standards.

7. To avoid making a mistake with the clippers, scissor the shape of the diamond before you clip. Scissor the front half of the diamond shape first. Start at the partline at Point 1, half-way between the top and underside of the dog. Scissor up to Point 3 (**H**). Scissor the other side, from Point 2 up to Point 3, the same way. Now scissor the back half of the diamond shape. Start at Point 1 and scissor down to Point 4 (**I**). Scissor the other side, from Point 2 down to Point 4 the same way. Use the # 10 blade to clip out the diamond (**J**). When the diamond is completely clipped, if the distance from Point 3 to Point

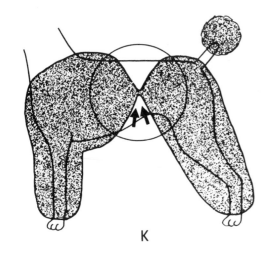

K

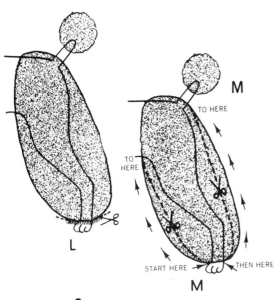

L

TO HERE

TO HERE

M

START HERE   THEN HERE

M

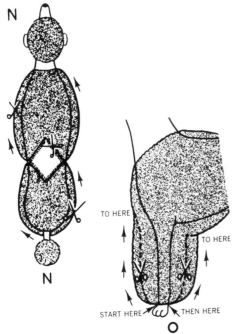

N

TO HERE

TO HERE

START HERE   THEN HERE

N

O

4 measures two to three inches on Toy Poodles, four inches on Miniature Poodles and six to eight inches on Standard Poodles, the pattern is in proportion. To emphasize the diamond shape, use the # 10 blade to clip each side of the dog below Points 1 and 2 (**K**).

8. Stand the Poodle with his hindquarters facing you. Comb the hair on the back legs up and out. Shape the leg in the familiar pantaloon style. Scissor off any hairs that fall below the clipped line around the ankle (**L**). Then begin shaping the leg. The easiest way to scissor the pantaloon shape is to begin at the ankle and work up to the hip, stopping at the point where the leg joins the body. Scissor one part of the leg from the ankle up to the hip, then begin again at the ankle and scissor another part up to the hip. Work completely around the leg (**M**), until you have the desired shape. Follow the dog's natural conformation and show the angulation above the hock joint and the curve of the stifle joint. To scissor the hard-to-reach areas on the inside of the back leg, lift the opposite leg with your free hand. Scissor the other back leg. Make the legs even in size and shape.

9. Comb the hair on the hips, hindquarters, ribs, shoulders and chest to fluff out the coat. Always use the comb in an upward and forward motion to lift the hair, rather than flatten it. Begin body scissoring by shaping the hindquarters round, following the natural contours of the body. Scissor the hair to an even length. When scissoring near the cut-out diamond shape, comb the hair forward and scissor any hair that falls over the clipped lines to emphasize the pattern (**N**). Scissor the hair under the chest to the same length as on top. Turn the Poodle around to stand facing you. Scissor the front of the chest round, from shoulder to shoulder. Comb the hair near the clipped part of the neck. Scissor any hair that falls over the clipped line around the neck, to make the pattern look neat.

10. Comb the hair on the front legs. Scissor any hair that falls below the clipped line around the ankle. Then begin shaping the leg. Start at the ankle and scissor part of the leg up to the elbow. Begin again at the ankle and scissor another part of the leg up to the elbow. Work completely around the leg (**O**), until you have the desired shape. To scissor the hard-to-reach areas under the front leg, lift the leg and pull it gently forward to avoid cutting holes in the coat. Scissor the other front leg. Be sure both legs are even in size and shape.

11. Select any topknot style.

12. Select any ear style.

Variations of the Diamond Clip

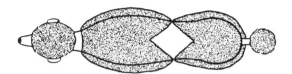

*Use the Diamond Body Pattern for
all of these variations.*

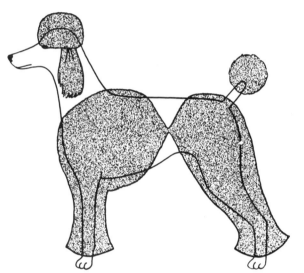

THE BELL-BOTTOM DIAMOND
(See Page 97)

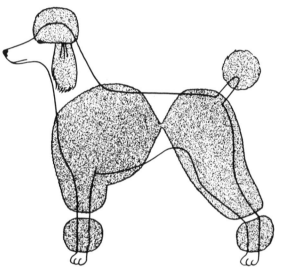

THE BOLERO DIAMOND
(See Page 98)

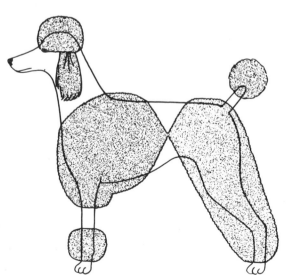

THE FIFTH AVENUE DIAMOND
(See Page 99)

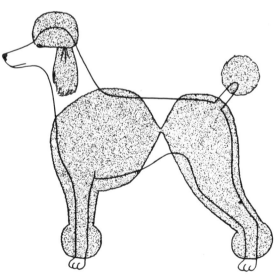

THE MIAMI DIAMOND
(See Page 100)

The Solitaire

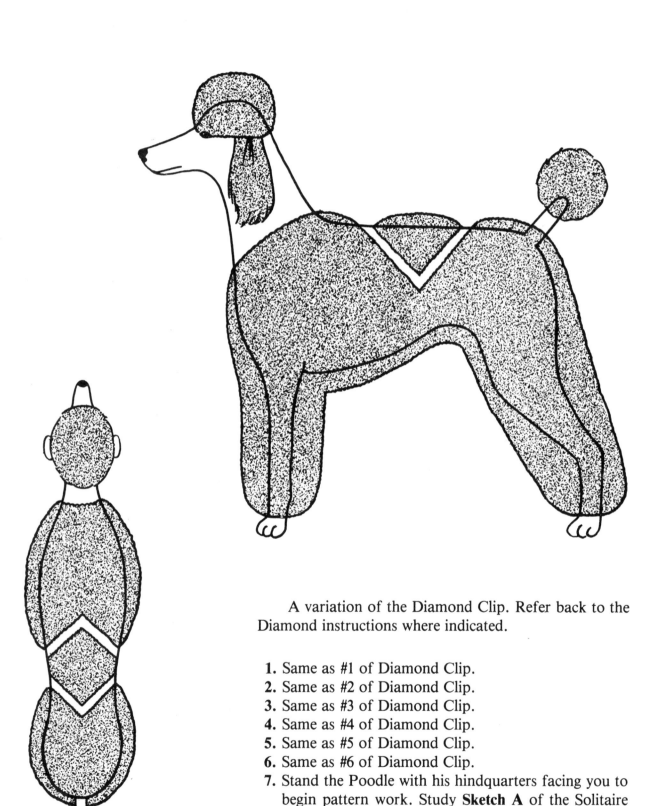

A variation of the Diamond Clip. Refer back to the Diamond instructions where indicated.

1. Same as #1 of Diamond Clip.
2. Same as #2 of Diamond Clip.
3. Same as #3 of Diamond Clip.
4. Same as #4 of Diamond Clip.
5. Same as #5 of Diamond Clip.
6. Same as #6 of Diamond Clip.
7. Stand the Poodle with his hindquarters facing you to begin pattern work. Study **Sketch A** of the Solitaire Clip. Points 1 and 2 must be at the last rib, half-way between the top and underside of the dog. Points 3 and 4 must be in the center of the back. Use chalk to mark

152

Points 1 and 2. Mark a dot on each side of the dog at the last rib, half-way between the top and underside of the body (**B**). Use chalk to mark Point 3. Mark a dot in the center of the back (**C**), two inches in front of the last rib on Toys, three inches in front of the last rib on Miniatures and four to five inches in front of the last rib on Standards. Use chalk to mark Point 4. Mark another dot in the center of the back, as shown in the same sketch, two inches in back of the last rib on Toys, three inches in back of the last rib on Miniatures and four to five inches in back of the last rib on Standards.

8. Use a #⅝ blade on Toy Poodles, a #⅞ or #⅝ on Miniatures and a #10 on Standards. Clip a strip from Point 3 to Point 2 (**D**). Then clip a strip from Point 3 to Point 1, as shown in the same sketch, to complete the front part of the diamond shape. Clip a strip from Point 2 to Point 4 (**E**). Then clip a strip from Point 1 to Point 4, as shown in the same sketch, to complete the back part of the diamond shape. Comb the hair on the inside diamond and scissor around the clipped lines to emphasize the shape of the diamond solitaire.

9. Same as #9 of Diamond Clip.
10. Same as #10 of Diamond Clip.
11. Same as #11 of Diamond Clip.
12. Same as #12 of Diamond Clip.
13. Same as #13 of Diamond Clip.

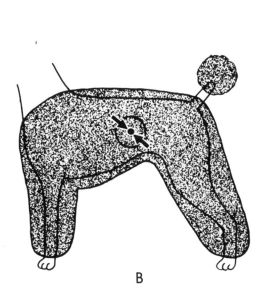

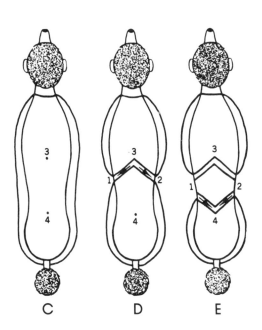

Since this is a different body pattern, you may use the Bolero, Bell-Bottom, Fifth Avenue, Miami and Saddle leg styles for five new variations of this clip.

The Mink Collar Clip

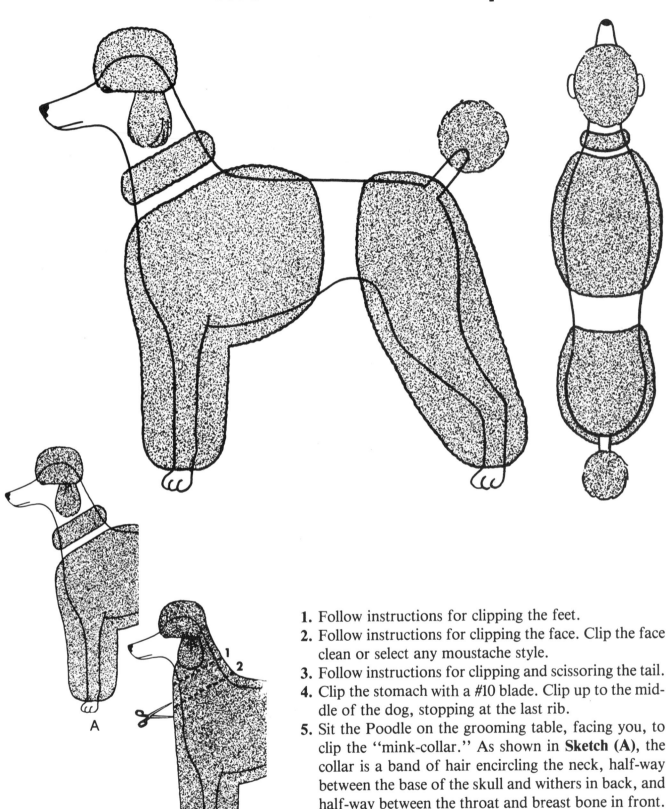

1. Follow instructions for clipping the feet.
2. Follow instructions for clipping the face. Clip the face clean or select any moustache style.
3. Follow instructions for clipping and scissoring the tail.
4. Clip the stomach with a #10 blade. Clip up to the middle of the dog, stopping at the last rib.
5. Sit the Poodle on the grooming table, facing you, to clip the "mink-collar." As shown in **Sketch (A)**, the collar is a band of hair encircling the neck, half-way between the base of the skull and withers in back, and half-way between the throat and breast bone in front. The collar should be about three-fourths of an inch wide on Toy Poodles, one to one and one-half inches wide on Miniature Poodles, and two to two and one-half inches wide on Standard Poodles.

154

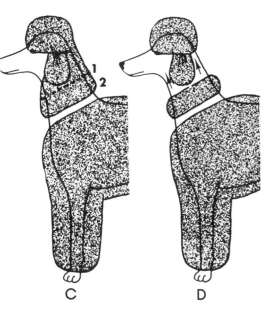

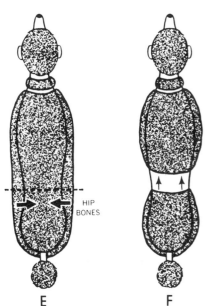

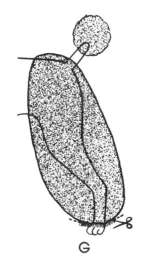

Before using the clippers, cut lines 1 and 2 with scissors (**B**), to avoid making a mistake. Then use a #10 blade. Start clipping the back of the neck first. Pointing the clippers upward, start at the shoulders and clip to line 2. Continue clipping around the neck by working from the shoulders up to line 2. Each side of the neck is clipped from the shoulder bone to line 2. The front of the neck is clipped from just above the breast bone to line 2. As shown in **Sketch (C)**, the collar is half completed.

6. Start again at the back of the neck, this time at line 1. Pointing clippers upward, clip from line 1 up to the base of the skull. Clip around the neck from line 1 in this same manner, until you have completed the collar (**D**).

7. Stand the Poodle with his hindquarters facing you to begin clipping the body. About one inch in front of the hipbones on a Toy Poodle, one and one-half to two inches in front of the hipbones on a Miniature and from two to three inches in front of the hipbones on a Standard, use a comb to make a part across the back (**E**). This part must be in front of the hipbones in the center of the back, and forward of the spot where the back legs join the body on each side of the loin. If you make the part at the hipbones, the hindquarters will appear weak. With a #10 blade, start at the part and clip to the last rib, until you have clipped a wide band around the dog's middle (**F**). Be sure the clipped lines around the hips and ribs are straight and that there are no straggly hairs on the dog's middle.

8. Stand the dog with the hindquarters facing you. Comb the hair on the back legs up and out to fluff the coat. The leg shape is the popular pantaloon style. Scissor off any hairs that fall below the clipped line around the ankle (**G**). Then begin shaping the leg. The easiest way to scissor the pantaloon shape is to begin at the ankle and work up to the hip, stopping at the point where the leg joins the body. Scissor one part of the leg from the ankle up to the hip. Then begin again at the ankle and scissor another part up to the hip. Work completely around the leg until you have the desired shape (**H**). Remember to emphasize the Poodle's natural angulation at the stifle and hock joints. Always hold the scissors flat against the hair you are working on. Do not dig into the coat with scissor points. Do not pull the hair out with your fingers. If you are not satisfied with the leg shape, recomb the part you are working on and

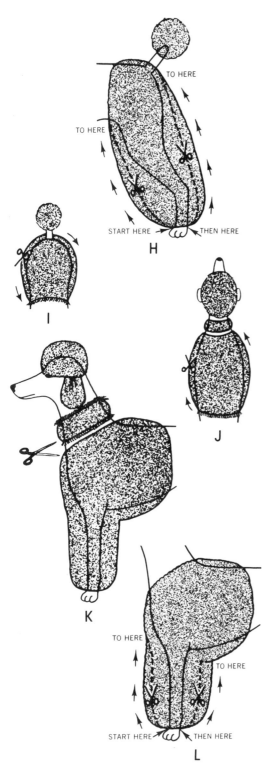

begin scissoring again. To scissor the hard-to-reach areas on the inside of the back leg, lift the opposite leg with your free hand. Leave the same amount of hair on both sides of the legs. Scissor the opposite back leg. Be sure both legs are even in size and shape.

9. Comb the hair on the hips and hindquarters. Shape the hindquarters round with the scissors, following the natural contours of the dog's body. When scissoring the hair near the clipped line around the hips, comb upward and forward, then scissor off any hair that falls over the clipped line to make the pattern look neat (**I**).

10. Comb the hair on the ribs, shoulders and chest. Scissor any hair that falls over the clipped line at the last rib to emphasize the pattern (**J**). Scissor the jacket to the same length as the hindquarters, following the natural contours of the body. Scissor the hair under the chest to the same length as on top. Turn the dog around to stand facing you, and shape the front of the chest round, from shoulder to shoulder. Comb the hair at the clipped line from the withers to the breast bone. Scissor off any hair that falls over the clipped part. Comb the hair at lines 1 and 2, and scissor around each line to make the mink-collar look neat (**K**).

11. Comb the hair on the front legs. Scissor off any hair that falls below the clipped line around the ankle. Then begin shaping the leg. Start at the ankle and scissor one part of the leg up to the elbow. Begin again at the ankle and scissor another part of the leg up to the elbow. Work completely around the leg, as shown in **Sketch L**, until you have the desired shape. If you are not satisfied with your scissor work, recomb the area you are working on and begin scissoring again. To scissor the hard-to-reach areas under the front leg, lift the leg under which you want to scissor and pull it gently forward to avoid cutting holes in the coat. Scissor the other front leg. Make both legs even in size and shape.

12. Select any topknot style with the Mink Collar Clip.

13. Select any ear style.

NOTE: For six variations of the above Mink Collar Clip, use the Bolero, Bell-Bottom, Fifth Avenue, Miami, Continental and Saddle leg styles. Instructions for these variations begin on Page 97.

You may also clip a Mink Collar on the following patterns: the Sporting, the Miami, the New Yorker, the Dutch, the Chicago Dutch, the Pittsburgh Dutch, the Royal Dutch, the Criss-Cross Dutch, the Sweetheart, the Bandero, the Rio Bandero, the Diamond, the Solitaire, the London Continental, the Spanish Continental, the Roman Continental and each of variations of these patterns for *a total of 73 additional clips.*

156

FINISHING TOUCHES

Finishing touches—nail polish and bows—are strictly a matter of personal preference. Many pet owners like to paint the nails or add bows to match their Poodle's collars and leashes while others feel these are rather decadent practices.

Nail Polish

If you wish to color your pet Poodle's nails, use an epoxy enamel made for dogs and not a human nail polish. Most pet and department stores stock several brands of dog nail polish which come in a variety of colors, are quick-drying and will not chip off easily.

1. Apply a coat of nail polish on the nails of one foot, keeping your Poodle's toes separated as you brush on the enamel.
2. Even though epoxy polishes are quick drying, some dogs become fussy while their nails are painted and the polish smears over the paw. One way to prevent this from happening is to use a nail enamel fast drying spray formulated for human nails. These products stop smudging and surface dry the polish quickly without leaving a dulling film. They are as effective on dog nails as on human nails. Hold the can about 4 inches from the nails and gently spray in a slow arc. Remember to keep the spray away from the dog's face.
3. Do the other feet as instructed.

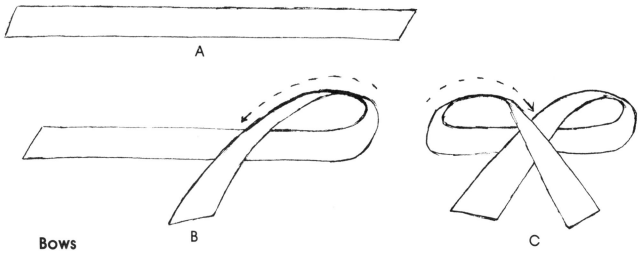

A

B   C

Bows

Everyone has his or her favorite way of making hair bows, but you can make one in a few seconds (that will stay firmly attached to the hair when applied correctly), by following these directions:

1. Start with a piece of ribbon from 8 to 14 inches long, as shown in **Illustration A**. The length of the ribbon depends on the size of the Poodle that will wear the bow. Generally, a 6 to 8-inch long ribbon makes a balanced bow for Toys; a 10 to 12-inch ribbon is sufficient for Miniatures, and a 14-inch ribbon or slightly longer is best for Standards.
2. Fold the right end of the ribbon to the center to make a loop on the right side, as shown in **Illustration B**, holding the loop in place with your fingers.
3. Fold the left end of the ribbon to the center, making a loop on the left side, as shown in **Illustration C**, and hold both loops in place with your fingers.

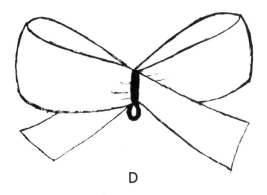

D

4. With your free hand, twist a small latex or rubber band around the center of the bow, as shown in **Illustration D.** (One end of the latex band loops through the other and holds the bow in place.) It might take a little practice to pass one end of the band through the other but, with a little dedication, you can do it easily. If you have difficulties at first, use a tiny staple or stitch to hold the ribbon together before applying the band.

This kind of bow can be applied easily to topknots, ears or other parts of the coat by the loop of the band that holds the ribbon together. To apply an ear bow, pull out a few strands of the long feathering at the top center of the Poodle's ear. Place the loop of the latex band around this small section of hair and twist it around the feathering once again to hold it in place. **Photograph 1** shows ear bows attached.

Bows attached to the hair in this manner will not injure the ear leather or damage the feathering and will stay firmly attached until the band is snipped with scissors. **Photograph 2** shows a Poodle with bracelet bows attached the same way.

For a really elegant look, use two pieces of ribbon in harmonizing colors or one solid-one plaid to make each bow. You may also use brightly colored yarn in place of ribbon. For a pretty and soft touch, after the yarn bow is attached, use a fine comb to carefully comb out the end pieces of yard.

1

2

Across the Ocean

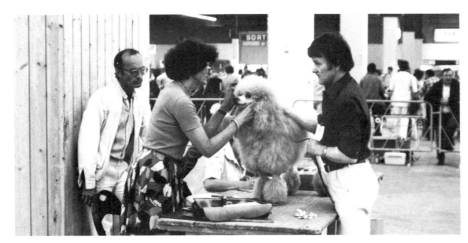

Poodle judging at the Paris dog show, France.

At left, silver Miniature Poodle (*Caniche Moyen*) in "Lion" clip waits at ringside at the *Europeenne et Internationale Exposition Canine*, Paris, France. Right, headstudy of the same Poodle. In some European countries, particularly France, the topknot on a show clip is not tied up as it is in the United States and England. Instead, the topknot resembles our pet trim styles, but it is slightly longer, shaped somewhat round and brushed upward. A moustache is permitted.

Miniature Poodle in the "Penny" clip in a grooming salon in Brussels, Belgium. This style is similar to our "Kennel" clip. The feet usually are not clipped (only hair between the pads is removed) but shaped round with scissors instead.

White Miniature Poodle from the Netherlands in "Lion" clip.

White Standard Poodle, Best of Utility Group at Crufts Dog Show, London, 1981.

Silver Miniature Poodle in Continental trim being prepared for the show ring in England.

An exhibitor applies finishing touches to his white Standard Poodle in English Saddle clip at the Crufts Dog Show in London.

Miniature Poodle in Puppy Clip being judged at the Crufts Dog Show. This style is usually seen on older puppies in England. Notice the scissoring on the hindquarters.

Black Miniature Poodle from Germany trimmed in the most popular pet trim on the Continent. It is called the "Pantalon" or "Zazou" clip in France and Belgium, and the "Nia Schur" in Germany, Austria and the Netherlands.

An unbrushed white Belgian Poodle in the "Pantalon" clip. The feet may be either shaved or left unclipped and scissored round. The ears may be left full or all the feathering can be clipped off. The tail pompon is optional.